Mindfulness, Meditation and Self Development

Dr Michael Hewitt

Edited by Juliet Dover

THE NOTE TREE
www.thenotetree.com

All rights reserved. No part of this publication may be reproduced, distributed, or transmitted in any form or by any means, including photocopying, recording or other electronic or mechanical means, without the prior written permission of the publisher, except in the case of brief quotations embodied in critical views and certain other uses permitted by copyright law.

The meditation exercises given in this book are those which have worked for the author, however should you choose to try any of the exercises herein there are no guarantees that they will work in the same way for you. Meditation is generally a very safe activity to engage in, particularly during the early stages of learning to meditate. However, as one's practice advances a process of self-examination will begin. Should you not wish to engage in this process, then please confine your practice to those exercises presented in the first six chapters of this book.

If you have any history of any kind of mental illness you should not try to practice any of the meditation exercises in this book without first obtaining the direct agreement of your mental health care provider who will provide you with the necessary supervision. This will ensure that your practice is sympathetic and augmentative to any course of action or treatment your mental health carer may be recommending for you.

The views and opinions expressed in this book are those of the author. Consequently, they should not be treated as a substitute for professional medical advice. Any use of the information in this book is therefore at the reader's discretion and risk. Neither the author nor publisher can be held responsible for any loss, claim or damage arising from the use or misuse of the information herein, the reader's failure to take medical advice or for material represented on third party websites.

Copyright © 2015 by Michael Hewitt

Cover illustration by Olivier Le Moal,
licensed courtesy of www. Gograph. com

Cover design by Ashley Hewitt

First printing: 2015

ISBN:095754703X
ISBN-13: 9780957547032

DEDICATION

To my son Ashley Hewitt

CONTENTS

0	Introduction	1
1	Windows to Presence	5
2	Mindfulness and Mental Cultivation	19
3	The Art of Anticipation	25
4	Walking with Presence	34
5	Working with Presence	41
6	Mindfulness as a Way of Life	47
7	Preparing for Formal Meditation	50
8	Breath Meditation	60
9	More Advanced Meditation Techniques	68
10	Visualization	75
11	Creative Visualization	87
12	The Beautiful Place Exercise	98
13	The Art of Mimesis	109
14	A Higher Level of Mindfulness	117
15	A Meditation Toolkit	125
16	Contemplation	138
17	Dwelling	153
18	Meditation	166
19	Meditation as a Way of Life	173
	Bibliography	180

INTRODUCTION

The intention of this book is to take the reader on a journey of exploration into the fascinating world of meditation – what it is, how to do it and what a person might seek to achieve through learning to meditate.

My interest in meditation first began many years ago when living and working in central London. Like many other young people, I was looking for ways to maintain a sense of inner calm amidst the rushed, chaotic and often stressful hustle and bustle of city life.

Having heard about the benefits of meditation from friends and acquaintances who were both keen and expert practitioners, I decided to give it a try. I first began practicing various meditation and mindfulness techniques under the guidance of qualified teachers and then later, branching out on my own, put into practice everything that I had learned.

When I started out, I was simply an ordinary person who tried meditation, found it rewarding, and as a result, continued with the practice. Since then my practice has grown and matured to the point that it is now an integral part of my life - in fact I could not now imagine what it must be like not to meditate. In this respect these years of study have placed me in a good position to write about and explain both the practice and the benefits of meditation.

This book is for those who are seeking an introduction to the arts of meditation, what they are and how to practice them. As such, the book is written in an instructional format that is addressed to a would-be meditation practitioner. In this sense, it offers a basic course in the arts of meditation.

In order to follow this course, no prior experience of meditation is needed. Furthermore, no religious or spiritual beliefs are either assumed on behalf of the practitioner, or needed by the practitioner in order to learn the arts discussed in this book. This is because the arts of meditation are always very practical and as such, do not depend upon subscription to any particular belief system. In this sense, meditation can be learned by anybody who takes an interest in doing it, irrespective of their own particular beliefs, religion or spiritual path.

The structure of this book reflects the two main types of meditation practice that are currently recognized in the West. These are mindfulness meditation, which is concerned with the day to day cultivation of a certain frame of mind, and contemplative meditation, which is ordinarily undertaken seated in a particular space that has been prepared for it.

Although both types of meditation are catered for in this introduction, the book will begin with the former, for the simple reason that mindfulness practice represents an excellent foundation for contemplative meditation generally.

Concerning the latter, the practice of contemplative meditation will be broken down onto four levels which are visualization, contemplation, dwelling and meditation. These refer to the four most well-known, safe, tried and trusted techniques for contemplative meditation.

As such, overall this book will cover five basic techniques of meditation, for each of which a number of specific exercises will be given, both within the chapters and in a shorter form at each chapter's end. Through the practice of these exercises, it will then become possible to learn the basics of each technique. Once learned, you will then be better equipped to pursue your own meditative journey, concentrating and focusing upon whichever techniques appeal to you the most.

In doing so, please be aware that this book is simply an introduction to the arts of meditation and the expert guidance of a qualified instructor should be sought should you wish to delve much more deeply into the practice of meditation.

When working through this book bear in mind that progress in meditation tends to occur in a slow, steady and gradual manner. For this reason, there is no point expecting quick or immediate results. Instead, try working through each chapter one at a time, practising and studying the exercises, not going on to the next chapter until you feel you have learned the techniques being taught.

In terms of the time it takes you to do this, it does not really matter. By taking your time in this fashion, you will be learning exactly what you set out to learn in the first place.

Having said this, let us now proceed to the study of meditation, which will begin with the study of mindfulness practice.

1 WINDOWS TO PRESENCE

Meditation literature abounds with references to particular techniques of meditation, so much so in fact, that one could easily be forgiven for thinking that the key to meditation all lies in the particular technique that is used. However, despite what anybody might believe to the contrary, one of the most vital elements of meditation is not so much *what* you are doing i.e. in terms of the technique itself, but your exact *state of mind* as you are doing it. How aware are you? How focused and present are you?

In other words, in order to be able to meditate, a certain state of mind is desirable. From this it therefore follows that any activity undertaken in order to specifically cultivate that state of mind, is by rights a kind of meditation. It may not share many of the outward characteristics of formal types of meditation, which are usually undertaken seated in a specially prepared space for them. But it will certainly count as an informal type of meditation.

Informal types of meditation are just as important in their own way as formal types, even if only for the reason that they offer vital practise in developing those important abilities and states of mind that are needed to be able to successfully practice formal types of meditation. One such vital ability, with which the first few chapters of this book will be concerned, is the ability to be mindful.

The terms mindfulness meditation or alternatively, mindfulness techniques refer to those exercises that you can practice in order to specifically cultivate this quality of mindfulness. A person who practices these, is therefore said to be engaged in mindfulness practice.

In recent years the practice of mindfulness has started to become very popular. This is for very good reason. Mindfulness is not only a good preparation for meditation practice generally, but even if they do not go on to study more advanced levels of meditation, it can also bring great benefits to the practitioner.

The benefits of mindfulness practice have been appreciated in the East for thousands of years, being integral to numerous Eastern religious and spiritual paths, such as Buddhism, Zen Buddhism and Taoism. Due to the increasingly powerful influence of such paths on contemporary Western culture, an awareness of the great value and benefits of mindfulness is also now making itself increasingly felt in the Western world as well.[1]

Studies have shown that mindfulness practice can have many beneficial effects upon the practitioner's

---

[1] Although commonly recognized as having a Buddhist origin, practices that are similar to or directly related to mindfulness are present in many other traditions as well. These include the monastic Christian tradition, Sufism, Kabbalah, the Western Hermetic tradition and the Fourth Way as popularised by the Russian writer Ouspensky.

psychological well-being.[2] The practice has further been shown to be capable of reducing a person's blood pressure, calming anxiety, alleviating depression, eliminate unnecessary worrying and to act as a general panacea against many of the unfortunate mental and psychological ills that tend to afflict people living in modern society.[3]

In this sense, mindfulness as practiced in the West is often pursued independently of any religious or spiritual pathway, for no other reason than its intrinsic health benefits.[4] As a long term practitioner of mindfulness I can personally attest to the fact that that in addition to the many benefits outlined above, regular practise also leads to a heightened sense of awareness, increased levels of energy and concentration and a clarity of mind that results in improved levels of performance in virtually every sphere of life. Because of this, the practice of mindfulness may be recommended to everybody, irrespective of whether or not they pursue a religious or spiritual pathway[5]

---

[2] Brown, Kirk Warren; Ryan, Richard M (2003), *The Benefits of Being Present: Mindfulness and its Role in Psychological Well-being.*

[3] P. Grossman; L. Niemann, S. Schmidt. (2004). *Mindfulness-based Stress Reduction and Health Benefits: a Meta Analysis.*

[4] As practiced in this context therefore, mindfulness does not necessarily carry the same ethical connotations as it does in say Buddhism, where it is practiced from the more integrated perspective of the Noble Eightfold Path.

[5] A popular course on Western mindfulness is Professor Mark William's (2011) *Mindfulness: A Practical Guide to Finding Peace in a Frantic World.*

WHAT IS MINDFULNESS?

Mindfulness entails placing the focus of one's awareness non-judgmentally upon the present moment. This sounds simple enough, but what does it actually involve? Here it is helpful to realize that there are certain activities that require a mindful state in order to be able to do them properly. A good example of this is the Chinese art of Tai Chi.[6]

In order to be able to appreciate some of the qualities of mindfulness, spend some time observing the way in which expert Tai Chi practitioners complete each movement in a deliberate, focussed and unhurried fashion. The practitioners will not be thinking about what they had for dinner last night or a date that they might be going on next week. Their mind will be fully focused upon the present moment as expressed through the particular movement that they are performing.

This alert state of *presence* is one of the integral features of mindfulness. And within it there lies a great sense of mental freedom, expansion and release. For in mindfulness we shift the focus of the mind away from our problems and instead, enter into and experience a liberating state of presence. This in turn then enables us to connect directly with the tremendous power of the present moment.[7]

---

[6] See Hine, J. (2014), *Tai Chi and Mindfulness*.

[7] Eckhart Tolle's *The Power of Now* (1999) represents one of the most definitive expositions of this subject.

ABANDONING PRECONCEPTIONS

One of the greatest barriers to understanding meditation is having preconceived ideas of what it actually is. For example, if I ask you to picture a person meditating in your mind's eye, I can pretty much guarantee that you will picture somebody sitting upright in the lotus position with their eyes closed and perhaps even humming 'OM' to themselves.

The sooner such preconceptions can be abandoned the better. This is because in essence, meditation represents any conscious effort to change one's own mind state for the better. When a person takes a few deep breaths in order to calm themselves down prior to entering the room for a job interview they are practicing a form of meditation. Similarly, when an angry person steps back from the situation that they are in and counts to ten in order to calm themselves down, that is also a form of meditation.

Indeed, in order to meditate it is not even necessary for a person to sit down. They can be meditating by the way in which they complete a task. This is because the primary concern of meditation is not *what* you are doing, but *how* you are actually doing it. What is your state of mind? Are you present? What is the state of your being at that time?

Another vital feature of mindfulness is a willingness to let the present moment be as it is, without judgment, conditions or requirements that it be any different. In the literature of Tai Chi, this quality can be referred to by the words Wu Wei, which are often translated as meaning *non-action*.[8] However, these words do not mean *doing nothing*. They mean not getting in the way of the present moment, but instead allowing it to simply be as it is, without interference, control or judgment on our part. Wu Wei in this sense, is both a guardian and gateway to the richness and fullness of the experience of true presence.

MINDFULNESS PRACTICE

Reading about a state of mindfulness is one thing, while coming to know and experience it for oneself is another. Indeed, you could read many books about mindfulness and still not grasp what it is. This is because the only way to know mindfulness is through doing and experiencing it. Initially, this experience may be gained through practice of informal meditation exercises that have been specifically developed for the purposes of developing mindfulness. Some short and simple exercises suitable for this purpose are given at the end of this chapter.

These are based on the observation that mindfulness is not difficult to learn provided that one starts small efforts. To do otherwise is to risk taking on too much at the very beginning, thereby making some of the

---

[8] Slingerland, E. (2006), *Effortless Action: Wu Wei as Conceptual Metaphor and Spiritual Ideal in Early China*

difficulties encountered seem to be insurmountable. By starting small, some kind of success is guaranteed from the outset. From this perspective therefore, the path to mindfulness then becomes a matter of each small success building upon the previous success.

In this respect, each such effort to be mindful, no matter how small, will always count. No single effort is ever wasted on the path to mindfulness and eventually these efforts will build up into something that is capable of having a powerfully transformative effect upon your life.[9]

This is because the more often they are practised, the more deeply a liberating and fulfilling state of presence will begin to be experienced, opening a doorway to a richness and fullness of experience that is profoundly rewarding and healing for the mind.

This all begins with the small: learning how to fully appreciate the supreme gift that is the present moment, a gift that is given to all of us, every single second of our lives.

WINDOWS TO PRESENCE

A useful method for doing this is called windows. We understand a window to be a space in the wall that lets in the light from outside. In mindfulness meditation, the windows are those created in order to let the light of presence shine through into our lives.[10] These take the form of small, short exercises where the aim is to

---

[9] See Sylvia Boorstein,(1996). *Don't Just Do Something, Sit There: A Mindfulness Retreat with Sylvia Boorstein*

[10] Presence in the sense of the reality of the present moment.

focus your attention non-judgementally upon what is happening in the present moment.

One such exercise for example, is called the heron. Perhaps you have seen herons standing patiently, but alertly, on the edge of a pool waiting for a fish to come by. In this exercise you are required to imagine that you are a heron, except that the pool in this case is your mind, while the fish are the thoughts that might come into your mind. All that the exercise involves therefore, is spending a minute or so carefully watching your own mind, waiting for the next thought to pop into your head.

Try it now. Look up from reading this book and spend the next minute or so watching your mind alertly like a heron watching out for fish.

Having done this exercise, then ask yourself, who or what was doing the watching? Ordinarily, we tend to identify ourselves with our thoughts. Therefore if we are thinking unhappy thoughts, we then tend to find ourselves beginning to feel unhappy as a result. However, if we were truly no more than a reflection of our own thoughts, how could we then be capable of standing back and watching out for those thoughts, like a heron watching out for fish?

Another such exercise is called audition. For this exercise you are required to suddenly stop whatever you are doing and - for about one minute - listen very carefully to the sounds in your environment. When you hear a sound, don't try to judge, identify or analyse it, just allow yourself to experience those sounds.

Again, try this exercise now - stop reading and spend the next minute or so listening intently to all of the sounds occurring in your environment.

Having done this, you will discover that the process of listening intently opens up a gap in the flow of one's thoughts. And it is in this that the benefit lies. Once that gap has been opened, there is no room in one's mind for thoughts of depression, sadness, worry or fear. Through that small gap, it then becomes possible to discern the glimmer of a new sense of self, not as a reflection of one's own thoughts, but as an alert, aware and above all peaceful listening presence.

MINDFULNESS EXERCISES

Further short exercises for the development of mindfulness are found at the end of this chapter, all of which are in a similar vein, requiring no more than a minute or so of your time.

One of the great features of these exercises is that in many cases, they can be practised anywhere. In this respect, they are particularly useful in those situations that do no more than to steal our precious time away, such as waiting for an appointment, being stuck in traffic or queuing in a shop.

This time never need be wasted again. Instead it can always be used productively towards the purposes of being mindful.

There are a total of fourteen such exercises provided at the end of this chapter. One way of approaching these exercises is to undertake a different one each day, beginning with the first exercise on the first day and so on.

Practice this exercise at least once in the day, but preferably for as many times in the day that you can find the opportunity to do so. When you reach the end of the fourteen day cycle, start again from the beginning. Keep doing this until you have developed in yourself an initial sense of what it means to be present, even if only for a few brief moments.

As you do these exercises, be encouraged by the fact that they all call upon the use of innate abilities of the human mind. Because these abilities are innate, there is consequently no need to worry about the technicalities of any exercise. Through persistent effort over a period of time you will eventually find the way of it and it will then become as easy and natural for you as eating, drinking or breathing.

WINDOWS TO PRESENCE EXERCISES

1 Scrutiny: Spend a minute or so scrutinizing everything in the field of your visual awareness. Do not think about or reflect upon anything that you see. Simply observe everything as if it were the first time you had opened your eyes and seen anything.

*   *   *

2 Audition: Spend a minute or so listening carefully to all of the sounds that enter into the field of your auditory awareness. Do not think about any of the sounds that you hear or even try to identify them. Simply listen to them in an impartial and non-judgemental manner.

*   *   *

3 Touch and feel: Pick up an object that is close to hand. Feel that object with your fingers, sensing the different textures, shapes and sensations produced by it. Show no concern for what the object is or what it is for. Simply enjoy the kinaesthetic sensations that arise from feeling and touching the object.

*   *   *

4 Fragrances: Pick up a piece of food, bring it up to your nose and carefully smell its range of odours. Do not try to analyse these or identify them for what they are. Simply experience the range of odours coming off the food, as if smelling them for the first time.

5 Alien environment: When alone in the house or flat, spend some time walking around the house looking, feeling and sensing everything completely anew, rather as if it were an alien environment. Do not think about the experience, but simply focus your mind upon the experience itself.

* * *

6 Heron: Imagine being a heron, carefully scrutinizing a pool for the presence of small fish. The pool in this case is the mind, while the fish are the thoughts that might pop into the mind. Just like a heron, carefully watch the pool of your mind waiting for a thought to appear. If a thought does appear, simply observe it like a heron would observe a small fish beginning to swim into its strike range.

* * *

7 Birdsong: The next time you hear a bird singing, if you are clear to do so, stop for a few moments and focus all of your attention upon the birdsong. Listen to this song without any sense of judgement, thought or any attempt whatsoever to analyse what is being experienced.

* * *

8 Breeze: The next time a gentle breeze is felt, stop to experience that breeze in a new and appreciative way. Feel the sensations of the breeze upon the skin, the feel of the fresh air as it enters into the nostrils. Do not think about the experience at all, just enjoy the feeling of the breeze for what it is.

9 Taste: Find something to eat, say for example an apple. Eat it slowly and carefully, focusing your mind completely upon the various sensations produced by the eating the apple. Concentrate fully on these to the exclusion of everything else. Enjoy them as if eating that particular food for the first time ever.

* * *

10 Five pointed star: Stand up with your legs apart and arms extended straight, so that your body forms a five-pointed star. Then scan and feel for the centre point of that star. Once you have found that centre point, dwell upon it for a while with your mind whilst maintaining the star posture.

* * *

11 Tension Scan: Spend some time mentally scanning your whole body, beginning with the feet and gradually moving upwards. Feel for any sources of muscular tension. If any are found, consciously relax those muscles before moving on. When finished, sense the body as a whole to make sure that everything is relaxed.

* * *

12 Feeling Within: If clear to do so, suddenly stop whatever you are doing and focus inwardly upon how you feel at that moment. Once aware of this feeling, do not think about or try to analyse that feeling, just be aware of it, even if that feeling is negative or one of discomfort. Just be with and accept the feeling.

13 Sentry: Stand up straight with your feet together and arms by your side, like an alert sentry. Stare straight ahead with your eyes focusing upon nothing in particular. Try to sense and feel from within the effect of that posture upon your frame of mind.

*   *   *

14 Freeze: When and if clear to do so, suddenly freeze in whatever posture you find yourself in. Do not think about the posture, but rather sense what it feels like from within. Stay in that posture for about a minute or so, or if this is not possible, for as long as you can maintain it within that time period.

2 MINDFULNESS AND MENTAL CULTIVATION

Each of the exercises given in the last chapter offer a brief window into the experience of being present. As such, they are short, easy to perform and applicable to a wide variety of different situations that you might find yourself in.

There is not much point doing these exercises just once and then expecting to see some benefit from them, since it is the aggregate of regular practice over an extended period of time that then leads to a clear idea of what presence actually is. In this respect, the length of time it takes you to get to this stage doesn't matter. The important thing is to keep trying until the point of the exercises has been clearly grasped, even if it takes you months of diligent practice.

Once you do have a clear sense of what presence actually is, and if even only for a few brief moments at a time, have felt and enjoyed the experience of presence, it then becomes possible to think about where your practice might then lead. It will be leading towards the point where you then become capable of identifying and utilizing those opportunities for being present in the various different situations that you find yourself in.

Inevitably, this is more difficult, for the simple reason that your are not necessarily following proscribed exercises anymore. Instead your are learning how to take advantage of those opportunities that life will present you with to become more present. The heartening fact is that these opportunities are everywhere, for the simple reason that everything that happens to us does so in the present moment.

As the present moment is therefore all that there is, a state of presence is always possible provided that you remember to focus your attention upon what is happening in the 'now'. As long as you remember to devote some time to this during the course of your day, you will make good progress in your efforts to be more present.

Let us now consider a few simple examples of how this might apply.

If you are walking down the street and you hear a bird singing, stop for a moment and listen intently to the birdsong. Do not think about the song, just enjoy it for what it is, without any sense of judgment or analysis. If by the side of the road, you see some beautiful flowers growing, allow yourself to enjoy and appreciate the sheer beauty of those flowers. If you feel a warm breeze blowing, stop for a moment to feel and enjoy the sensations of the breeze as it gently caresses your skin.

Observe that in all of these cases you are not actually required to do anything. This perhaps is one of the most difficult features of present moment awareness to understand. We ourselves do not have to do anything.[11] All that is required is to give oneself up to the power of the present moment. When you do learn to surrender to the moment in this way, you may then realize that our lives are absolutely filled with such moments, many of which are bursting out with a sense of promise, hope, vitality, inspiration and beauty.

Enjoying and appreciating these moments we then wonder why we never noticed them before. Clearly it is in these moments that our true wealth as human beings lies. Consequently it is a great pity that in our desperate striving towards a better future, we frequently tend to overlook the treasures that are already all around us.

REMEMBERING TO BE PRESENT

At this early stage, *remembering to try to be present* can sometimes be a little difficult. One way of countering this tendency towards forgetfulness is to turn the cultivation of presence into a game of sorts, which makes it more interesting and memorable for the mind. This is particularly useful for younger learners.

One such game of this type is called *stardust*.

For the purposes of this game, imagine the present moment as a portal through which this magical, glittering stardust enters the world. You then imagine that you are a vessel capable of collecting this

---

[11] This is a perfect demonstration of Wu Wei or non-action.

stardust. As a part of the game, once you have collected a certain amount of stardust, you are then given certain powers which enable you to move on to the next level. The aim of the game is to collect as much of this magical, glittering stardust as possible. This is done by seeking out opportunities to be present whenever and wherever you can. The more that such opportunities are exploited, the more stardust will be collected.

One way of visualizing this is to close one's eyes and imagine oneself as a golden chalice or vessel. Then picture this vessel being slowly filled with a fine, silvery stardust. Although this represents no more than a convenient way of visualizing this game, bear in mind that the vessel represents the self, while the stardust represents the revitalizing energy of the present moment.

From this standpoint, a new sense of yourself, *as presence*, will then begin to grow in direct proportion to how much of your time you spend in a state of presence.

These are the terms of the game and this is the challenge that it presents.

MENTAL CULTIVATION

Once conscious efforts are being made towards the cultivation of presence, it then becomes useful to consider the implications of those efforts. One such implication is that any attempt to become more mindful represents an intention to be more proactive in the cultivation of one's own state of mind. This represents a significant step forward, for it means that you no longer intend to be the victim of those unfortunate states of mind that might have afflicted you in the past. Instead, you are now choosing to adopt a stance of direct responsibility for your own states of mind and the activities that take place therein.

Another implication is that efforts to be more mindful represent an expressed willingness to be open to new levels of awareness and experience. This in turn portends a significant change in one's mental perspective, from being a person at the mercy of their own fluctuating mental states, to someone who intends to develop and make full conscious use of the powers of their own mind.

Both such implications are signs of significant progress for they represent the first steps of an exciting journey of learning, exploration and discovery in the fields of *mental cultivation* in general.

A good way of looking at this process is through the ancient analogy of the chariot. Under the terms of this analogy, the horses that pull the chariot are your feelings and emotions, while the chariot itself represents your body. The rider of the chariot in this case, pulling the reins of the horses and directing where the chariot will go, is your mind.

Now it is clear that the chariot of an uncultivated mind is very difficult to direct in a truly purposeful and meaningful fashion. This is because the person's mental activities are mostly unruly, chaotic and disorganized. Consequently, it is only when a decision is made to gain some control and direction over those mental activities that it then becomes possible for the chariot to travel with much more deliberation and clarity of purpose.

The effort to be more mindful in this sense, represents an important first step towards the process of mental cultivation. In this respect, it should not be forgotten that the process of mental cultivation is advantageous to all possible spheres of human endeavour, whether these be religious or secular, spiritual or practical. This is because it teaches a person how to harness and direct the incredible powers of their own mind.

For this very reason, meditation is not, and never will be, a religion.[12] Although often used as an aid and adjunct to religious practice, meditation has always been very much concerned with the cultivation of the tremendous powers of the human mind.

Therefore whilst the practice of meditation will enable a person to advantageously apply those powers to their further spiritual progression within their own chosen path, discipline or religion, those powers could equally be cultivated and developed by an atheist, seeking to deepen their relationship with nature, or a business person wishing to use the powers of their mind in a more productive, effective and forthcoming fashion.

Meditation in this sense, can be advantageously practiced by everybody, irrespective of their faith, calling or creed.

---

[12] See Chopra, D. (2013) *Meditation has Nothing to do with Religion.*

3 THE ART OF ANTICIPATION

The last chapter discussed the possibilities of being more proactive in terms of seeking out opportunities to be more present. When trying to do this, bear in mind that it will not happen just because you want it to. Some prior thought may often be needed in order to be able to recognize and track down those opportunities as and when they arise. This is called the *art of anticipation*, for it is to anticipate the arrival of a particular situation and then make a decision to use that situation when it does arise as an opportunity to become more mindful.

This works particularly well for repetitive situations that you know will occur again in the future. Rather than get caught out by them and waste the opportunity that they will offer you to become more mindful, this chapter invites you to begin anticipating these situations so that when they do arise, you are already prepared for them.

A useful aid towards this end is a journal in which you can write about your efforts to become more present, reflect upon those efforts and note down any important observations about the process that might occur to you. In your journal you can also create an action plan in terms of future situations that you intend to use for the purposes of mindfulness practice.

A very productive exercise for this is to take note of those situations, events and happenings that are liable to crop up again in your immediate future. The key here is repetition. What have you done before that you are liable to do again?

A really simple example of this is drinking a cup of tea or coffee - something most of us may do several times a day. Knowing this, you then apply the art of anticipation. In your mind, you log with yourself that the next time that you drink your beverage that you will try to do so in a mindful way.

Consequently, when you do sit down for that beverage, rather than consuming it in the same unthinking way that you might have done before, you can then turn the action of drinking it into an opportunity to be more mindful.

Let us look at how to go about this.

First of all, it would be advisable to stop and slow down for a moment. If necessary take a few deep breaths. And then when you are ready, begin to drink the beverage in a calm and focused manner. While doing so, rather than allowing yourself to drift off into pleasant daydreams, or a chain of unrelated thoughts give the drink your full and undivided attention. Focus your attention completely upon the action of drinking - the flavours, its aroma and warmth and the sensations that arise in you as you drink it. Above all enjoy it as if it were the first time that you had ever drunk this beverage.

Through use of the art of anticipation in this way, you

can thus learn how to become the conscious creator of your own opportunities to become more present.

Another good example of an event that is liable to happen again is say, eating a piece of fruit.

Rather than eating the fruit on auto-pilot as it were, instead turn the action of eating the fruit into an opportunity to be more mindful. Therefore eat the piece of fruit slowly and carefully, focusing your mind completely upon the various sensations produced by eating it. Concentrate fully on these to the exclusion of everything else. Enjoy them as if eating that particular food for the first time ever.

Another valuable arena in which to practice mindfulness is provided by our dealings with other people. Again these are often characterized by a certain sense of repetition in which similar situations keep cropping up over and over again.

A perfect example of this is having a conversation.

If you spend some time observing yourself as you converse with others you may find that much of the time you might be distracted, not listening properly, fidgeting with something whilst you are speaking, or only paying partial attention to the person doing the talking.

This is an ideal situation in which to practice mindfulness. Rather than allowing yourself to be distracted, instead try to give your full attention to the person with whom you are speaking. Listen intently to what they are saying, observe them carefully, and try to be alert to the micro expressions that cross their face as they converse with you. Be fully present for the conversation in other words, focussing upon that person and what they are saying to the exclusion of all else.

As you are conversing, try also to observe yourself and the ways that you are reacting to the conversation. However, rather than getting drawn into those reactions, try to stand back from them and watch them after the fashion of an impartial observer. It is surprising how much we can learn about ourselves by doing this.

Suffice to say, human conversation is a particularly productive area for mindfulness practice.

PORTALS TO PRESENCE

The pursuit of mindfulness can also be aided through the use of certain special portals to presence that unbeknown to most, are in fact everywhere around us. Anticipating these portals then enables one to be never caught out by having nothing to do.

Two very powerful portals in this respect are *space* and *silence*. As these do and can play such an important part in the pursuit of mindfulness, let us now consider them one at a time, beginning first of all with space.

When we walk into a room we inevitably focus our attention upon the people and objects in the room. This is understandable because they are the most powerful sources of stimulus that are presenting themselves to our senses. However, it is curious that we hardly ever focus upon something that in its own way, is just as important as the room itself. This is the space that everything in the room actually occupies.

Bearing this in mind, let us now consider some of the qualities of that space. The most obvious quality is its sense of complete and utter stillness. Space we may note, is always still and therefore also, very peaceful. Of course, what occupies a given space may not necessarily be still, but the space being occupied is always absolutely still, and in this sense, always totally peaceful.

Now by focussing our mind upon the qualities of that space, we will also see that space is supremely accommodating. It contains, upholds and embraces absolutely everything within itself, yet in itself calls for nothing. Because of this, space is actually a perfect expression of those very qualities of peace and stillness of mind that many meditation practitioners actively seek.

The point being made here, is that these qualities are forever present in each and every space that we enter into. Yet we never think to dwell upon or recognize these qualities. This in turn prevents us from realizing that actually, a peaceful state of utter stillness has been our constant companion throughout our lives. It was there when we were born, and it will be there when we die. In the meantime, it remains ever-present, awaiting no more than our recognition of the fact.

This then leads on to a curious thought. The fundamental backdrop to our entire existence is a silent and tranquil state of peace. The vastness of intergalactic space is a perfect physical expression of this. Now when we recognize this, we then see that our home planet Earth is a twinkling blue planet majestically coursing its way through a vast infinite ocean of complete and utter peace.

Knowing this, it then becomes apparent that at any moment of our lives, should we choose to do so, we may draw from that vast ocean of stillness and peace. All that needs to be done in this case, is for us to recognize and be mindful of it.

Try this now for a minute.

Spend a minute focussing your mind upon the peace and stillness of those quiet spaces that are within the room that you now occupy. By doing so, you will soon find that your mind then begins to become still and peaceful in response.

THE QUALITIES OF SILENCE

As if this were not enough, there is then the counterpart of the empty spaces to consider. This takes the form of a restful state of silence. Because space is perfectly still, no noise or sound is produced by it. The atmosphere that occupies that space may vibrate in such a way as to produce sound, but the space itself is always perfectly silent.

In this respect, it is interesting to see that every single sound always arises from a state of silence, to which it then always returns. Silence in this sense, is a perfect corollary for that peace and stillness of the empty void of space through which all things move.

Bearing this in mind, rather than always focussing upon any sounds that you hear, try instead focussing instead upon the spaces that occur between the sounds. Listen to the sounds carefully as they fade away to silence. And when they have faded away, listen carefully and try to focus intently upon the silence. You will find that silence tends to have the same effect upon the mind as the empty spaces. By focussing one's mind upon them, the mind then becomes still, peaceful and silent in return.

This is of course one of the major uses of singing bowls as used in the East. A type of standing bell, these bowls are designed to produce a long resonant tone that slowly fades away. By listening to that tone and following it on its journey back to silence, a mindful state is produced, one that is made all the more full when the tone has finally died away and there is nothing for the mind to dwell upon except for that peaceful state of silence.

THE ART OF ANTICIPATION EXERCISES

1 Beverage: Next time that you sit down to drink a cup of tea, coffee or other beverage, rather than drinking it in the same habitual way that you have always done before, turn the action of drinking it into a productive mindfulness exercise. Towards this end, slow down and stop for a moment and give yourself a chance to completely focus upon drinking the beverage. And then while you are drinking, rather than drifting off into pleasant daydreams or a chain of unrelated thoughts, instead focus completely upon the action of drinking it. Focus upon the flavours, the taste, the aroma, the warmth of the drink, the sensations that arise as you drink it. Above all enjoy it as if it were the first time that you had ever drunk that particular beverage.

* * *

2 Piece of fruit: The next time that you eat a piece of fruit, rather than eating it on auto-pilot, instead turn the action of eating the fruit into a mindfulness exercise. Therefore eat the piece of fruit slowly and carefully, focusing your mind completely upon the various sensations produced by eating it. Concentrate fully on these to the exclusion of everything else. Enjoy them as if eating that particular food for the first time ever.

3 Conversation: Start practising mindfulness as you converse with others. In order to do this, rather than allowing yourself to be distracted, instead give the person who you are conversing with your full attention. Listen intently to what they are saying, observe them carefully, and watch out for the micro expressions that cross their face as they are conversing with you. Be fully present for the conversation, focusing upon that person and what they are saying to the exclusion of all else. Truly listen to them in other words. As you are conversing, also observe yourself and the way that you are reacting to the conversation. Rather than getting drawn into those reactions, try to stand back from them and watch them as an impartial observer.

* * *

4 Peaceful spaces: Focus your mind for a minute or so upon the space that the room you are in provides an enclosure for. And then try to feel and sense its essential qualities. Feel its incredible sense of peace and utter stillness, the way in which space contains, upholds and embraces absolutely everything, yet in itself, calls for nothing.

* * *

5 Silence is golden: Rather than always focusing upon the sounds that you hear, spend some time focusing instead upon the silences or the spaces between the sounds. Listen to the sounds carefully as they fade away to silence. And when they do, listen carefully and try to focus your mind intently upon the silence itself.

4 WALKING WITH PRESENCE

As you continue with the practice of your mindfulness exercises, you will reach a point where you will then require some more demanding exercises, the practice of which will enable you to spend more of your time in a contented and peaceful state of presence.

An effective exercise in this category is the practice of *walking with presence*. As the title suggests, this treats the simple action of going for walk as a form of mindfulness meditation.[13] Although a very simple exercise, the benefits of treating walking as a form of meditation have been appreciated by meditation practitioners in one form or another for many millennia. One such benefit for the more experienced meditation practitioner is that walking with presence offers a refreshing contrast to processes of formal contemplative meditation, where it is often necessary to remain immobile for long periods of time.

Now ordinarily, walking tends to be a means to an end: we do it because we want to get somewhere and - judging by the pace at which most people walk - as fast

---

[13] One of the definitive guides to this art is *Walking Meditation* (2006) by Thich Nhat Hanh & Anh-Huong Nguyen.

and as quickly as possible. Because of this, walking is something that tends to be done on auto-pilot, i.e. as a very mechanical activity. This in turn leaves the mind free to then drift off into a stream of thoughts, random associations, daydreams and other such mental activities that do and can occur while a person is walking.

Now although there is nothing intrinsically wrong with walking in this fashion, both of these features signify a very low level of present moment awareness. Walking with presence aims to remedy both these tendencies, and instead turn the simple action of going for a walk into an ideal opportunity for entering into a deeper level of present moment awareness. For this purpose, the walk is not regarded as a means to an end, but is enjoyed and appreciated in and for itself.

Because of this, when walking with presence you try to place the focus of your attention not on thoughts of what happened yesterday or of what might happen tomorrow, but solely upon the experience of the walk itself.

This focus does and can include your bodily sensations such as the rhythmic swing of one's legs, the flexing of your muscles and the gentle rise and fall of your abdomen whilst breathing. It also includes trying to maintain an awareness of any thoughts that might pop into your mind whilst walking, and of course how you are actually feeling while on the walk. However, you try not to get involved in these, but simply to observe them as phenomenon rising up in the field of your awareness, in an impartial and non-judgmental manner

ALERTNESS AND AWARENESS

A good way to think about the sense of alertness and awareness associated with being present, is to think of a situation that would force one to become more alert and aware.

As an example of this, imagine being a lone astronaut whose craft had crash landed onto some strange planet. The onboard sensors indicate that the atmosphere is favorable to survival thereby making it safe to explore outside of the spacecraft. They further indicate the presence of many life-forms of unknown origins living upon this strange planet. Having crashed, it becomes vital to venture outside of the craft in order to try to obtain further supplies or perhaps to assess the exterior damage to the craft.

Imagine how you would feel stepping out of the craft and onto the surface of that planet for the first time. Every single one of your senses would be working at their maximum potential, thereby producing a heightened sense of alertness and awareness. This would include your sense of sight trying to make sense of the unfamiliar visual landscape; your sense of hearing trying to detect any sounds that might indicate the proximity of another life form and your sense of touch, feeling those sensations of coming into contact with the surface of the planet for the first time. In this case therefore, the situation itself would force you to become more fully *present*.

The exercise also calls for you to try to maintain a keen awareness of what is happening all around you as you walk. This includes enjoying and appreciating the beauty of the flowers and trees that you pass, the singing of the birds and the feel of the cool breeze on the skin.

Try also to be alert to the rare, the special, the unusual and the extraordinary events that may be transpiring around you, much of which often gets missed, because people are too busy checking their mobile phones or perhaps even daydreaming. These do and can include the curious activities of various creatures in the environment, the appearance of rare birds, or perhaps a particularly beautiful cloud formation.

One of the great features of walking with presence is that it can be performed anywhere, whenever there is an opportunity to go for a leisurely walk. However, because maintaining a state of presence can be very challenging at first, It is best to start off with small walks and then gradually build up from there. Towards this end, any short walk will admirably serve this purpose.

This now brings us to the consideration of one's attitude while walking. This is crucial because without the right attitude to the walk, the entire point of the exercise can be missed. Probably the best attitude is to think of yourself as being no more than a willing student of the present moment, for in this case the present moment then becomes your guide and teacher. This attitude is important, because it requires one to adopt a stance of receptivity to the present moment. In such a receptive state it is therefore possible to receive the maximum benefit from being present. This does and can include a direct connection to the incredible energy of the present moment, a willingness to learn the profound lessons that the present moment has to offer us and the opening up of a space in which it is possible for us to then be refreshed, healed and made new.

VARIATIONS ON A THEME

Walking with presence does not always have to be done in exactly the same way. There are many refreshing variations of the basic exercise of walking with presence, all of which can offer many interesting and fascinating insights into the potential depths of the exercise.

One such valuable exercise for example, is the slow motion walk.

As the name suggests this involves walking from one place to another in slow motion throughout. When doing this, there is a great risk that your efforts to walk in slow motion will be construed rather negatively by others. It is therefore a good idea to only perform the slow motion walk when you are clear and safe to do so, as for example when you are alone in the house.

Set the length of the walk, say for example from the kitchen up the bedroom, and then walk there in the slowest slow motion that you can maintain without losing your balance altogether. As you are walking, try not to get caught up in your thought processes. Instead, concentrate on the feelings and sensations that are arising in you as a result of walking in slow motion.

I could write for many pages about the beneficial effects of this exercise, although at this stage the important feature is for you to try it for yourself. It will cause you to experience the world in a completely different and altogether new way.

Another useful variation to try is the alternative gait.

All that this requires is for you to walk in a way that is different from your ordinary habitual way of walking. This could be by way of imitating somebody else's walk, or perhaps consciously altering one's stride pattern. It might involve remembering to hold one's head completely upright, or perhaps to move one's arms in a different way. The benefit of this, is that the necessity for remembering to maintain the alternative gait, keeps us anchored in the present moment.

However, in order to discover and appreciate the benefits of these exercises, it is necessary to go out and try them for yourself.

WALKING WITH PRESENCE EXERCISES

1 Mindful walking: Set aside some time for a mindful walk. This need not be a long walk. In principle, if it is possible to walk mindfully for a short walk, it can then be applied to longer walks. Before starting the walk, decide to focus exclusively upon the experience of the walk. This decision represents the mark of an intention not to get caught up in unrelated thought processes. If this happens, simply return one's focus back to the experience of the walk itself. Keep doing this as and when necessary.

*　　　　　*　　　　　*

2 Slow motion walking: This exercise is also best done in a private space where the walk will not be witnessed. The aim is to go on a short walk in slow motion. This deliberate slowing down of the pace of the walk not only causes a more mindful state, but it also brings what is happening within us into a much clearer perspective.

*　　　　　*　　　　　*

3 Alternative gait: The aim of this is to introduce a subtle change to the habitual manner in which you ordinarily walk. This change could be a deliberate lengthening of your stride, or perhaps moving your arms in a different way. The challenge lies in remembering to maintain the alternative gait, the effort towards which tends to keep us anchored in the present moment.

5 WORKING WITH PRESENCE

In a given day, each human being will do a tremendous amount of work, work in this case being defined as any activity undertaken in order to achieve a given outcome. Examples of work that fall within this definition are therefore activities such as clearing leaves from the patio, cleaning a room, washing the laundry, cooking a meal, building a wall, lighting a fire or any other type of activity that is undertaken in order to get a specific result.

Everybody has such jobs to do and in many cases, they can be a trial, especially those that are particularly tedious, exhausting or laborious. For the meditation practitioner, even the most difficult, challenging and obnoxious jobs represent a first class opportunity for the cultivation of presence.

Think therefore, what this means.

It means that the most menial tasks can be turned into powerful exercises for the cultivation of presence. It also means that all of the chores that attend one's daily life can then be transformed into dignified forms of expression of the art of meditation; each offering a wonderful opportunity to enter much more deeply into a state of presence.

This practice is called *working with presence.*

Given that you have already spent some time walking with presence, the requirements of working with presence will quickly become self-evident. This is because the skills that are brought into play when walking with presence are, in many cases, cross-transferable to other types of activity.

However, bear in mind that many of the tasks chosen for the working with presence exercise are by definition, goal oriented, and therefore require a particular outcome to be achieved within a certain time. It is therefore important to realize that some attitudinal adjustments will need to be made when working with presence.

POSITIVE ATTITUDES

For example, the first consideration is the task to hand. It does not really matter what the task is, the important qualification is the intention to consecrate that task to the cultivation of presence. Having consciously affirmed that decision, it is then necessary to try to complete the task as intended.

Something that will assist this is the maintenance of a supremely positive mental attitude towards the task itself. This acts as a useful guard against any negative feelings towards the task that might otherwise tend to sour the exercise, such as feelings of resentment at having to do it or thinking that the task is a waste of one's time.

Clearly it is not possible to work with presence if one is harboring negative feelings about the task. Therefore these need to be put to one side in order to maintain a supremely positive attitude towards the task to hand, an attitude which in itself will also bring with it great benefits. These do and can include a feeling of increasing enthusiasm towards the task, the generation of wave after wave of infectious positive energy and the arising within of a powerful sense of inspiration in the face of the tasks and challenges that life presents us with.

Another important attitudinal adjustment is the intention to commit oneself to working on the task with one hundred percent of one's capability. This is called working at maximum. Working at maximum represents a philosophy towards work that always brings out the very best of our capabilities. This is because it calls upon our best efforts and by so doing, brings the very best of us to bear upon the task.

By working at maximum, it is also possible to remain fully present. This is because when working at maximum there is no room in us for any ancillary processes, such as daydreaming or drifting off into a long chain of thoughts. Instead, every sense and sinew is being brought to bear and positively directed towards the completion and fulfillment of the given task.

In this respect, it is not really possible to be fully present, if you are somehow holding yourself in reserve. The question that arises from this is what is this reserve being held for? Some hypothetical ideal future that may not even arrive? Clearly in order to be able to work with presence it is necessary to recognize that this time has already arrived, and it is of course NOW. Not tomorrow when conditions might seem to be better. But NOW.

Working at maximum also ensures that we are always trying our very best. This in turn leads to significant improvements in our performance. These do and can lead to significant improvements in one's level of concentration, stamina, physical fitness, strength, resourcefulness, ingenuity and more. The result is not only a growing sense of self-enhancement, but it is also a case of success being heaped upon ever more success. The result is a positive surge of success that can then spread into other areas of one's life.

Another useful guideline is to always aim towards producing the highest possible quality of work. This is because it is not really possible to work with presence while working in a careless, slipshod manner that gives no heed or regard for the quality of the work.

Towards this end, allow yourself to be inspired by the great workers and craftspeople of the past who, striving toward excellence in their craft, created works of such superb quality, beauty and individuality that even today these works can inspire a state of presence in others who behold them.

EMANCIPATION FROM THE RIGORS OF LABOUR

One of the great benefits of working with presence is that it represents an ideal way to achieve internal emancipation from the rigors of labor. For it means that any task can be used as an opportunity for the cultivation of presence. With a little thought, care and resourcefulness therefore, any task, no matter how tedious it might seem, can be turned to one's advantage in this way.

However, because working with presence can be rather challenging, it is best to start off with very simple, easy tasks, such as peeling vegetables or perhaps washing the dishes. The positive advantages of this, is that these tasks thereby represent no more than a simple extension of those exercises that were given in chapter one.

Ordinarily, tasks such as those outlined above, may be looked upon as chores which means that they would ordinarily be performed in a very mechanical and humdrum way. With the right attitude however, all such chores can then be turned into effective exercises for the cultivation of presence.

If you have a pair of shoes to polish therefore, rather than resenting the task, or doing it in a half-hearted way, instead turn that task into a stately and dignified expression of the art of meditation.

Having gained some success with small jobs, it can then be applied to more lengthy tasks such as digging the garden or building a wall. With the right attitude, the most unenviable tasks can be turned into perfect opportunities for the cultivation of presence.

WORKING WITH PRESENCE

- *Decide upon a task. Begin small.*
- *Mentally consecrate that task to the cultivation of presence.*
- *Approach the task with a supremely positive mental attitude.*
- *Commit oneself to working at 100% of one's capability.*
- *Aim towards producing the highest possible quality of work.*
- *Focus only upon the experience of doing the work itself.*
- *Strive to be present at all times.*
- *When the task is finished, reflect upon the experience. How well did it go? Was there anything that could have been improved?*

6 MINDFULNESS AS A WAY OF LIFE

The preceding chapters of this book have demonstrated that that life presents us with many opportunities to become more mindful, provided that we are able to recognize and exploit these opportunities as and when they present themselves to us.

Towards this end, there are many useful concepts that act as pointers towards a more effective use of those opportunities.

One such pointer is the fact that life itself offers a steady succession of such moments, each of which bursts with a fullness of promise, inspiration and hope. With this in view, mindfulness then becomes less an exercise or a practice, and more a way of simply honouring the remarkable possibilities afforded to us by the present moment.

Another pointer concerns the lifting of the veil of familiarity that has so far prevented us from appreciating the value of the present moment. When that veil has been removed, we then become capable of seeing ourselves and the world with new eyes, that assist us to break away from those habitual patterns of thought that previously might have led us to depression or perhaps anxieties about the future.

Rather than being weighed down by such thoughts, we can instead learn to enjoy the freshness of the now and thereby become charged and empowered by those vibrant and re-vitalizing energies that always attend the present moment.

In this respect the present moment is rather remarkable in the sense that it is always completely and utterly new. Because of this, you could be living next to a river for your whole life for example, and there will never be a single moment in which that river was not somehow different to the way it was in the moment before.

In this way, the present moment is a direct gateway to a sense of newness, freshness and originality which, if we let it, will then grace and enhance us all of the days of our lives. Indeed, to engage like this is to be propelled towards that eternal now in which everything, no matter how small or great, is willingly participating. And it is to know that we ourselves have the honour and privilege of being part of that splendid moment.

Another concept relates to the arising of a new sense of honesty in the face of the present moment - not to any particular idea or principle - but towards our own mindful experience. There is a common assumption that whatever we are searching for nearly always lies in the future. Because of this we tend to fill the present moment with the stress of our continual striving towards this brighter and more hopeful future.

The question is: when does this future finally arrive? If we are honest with ourselves we will realize that it never really does. This is because, even when it seems to, we are too busy filling the present moment with the stress of our striving to create an even better future. In this way, by looking towards the future for our salvation, we then miss out on the true wealth of our human opportunity, which always lies in the present moment.

With such concepts in mind, we can more easily appreciate the fact that that the practice of mindfulness forever orients us towards the now, enabling us to become more fully present. This in its turn, allows us to enter into a rewarding state of presence in which we suddenly find ourselves freed from the constrictions and adverse results of our habitual thought patterns and feelings. From this point on therefore we can begin to cultivate that state of presence as a new way of life, one that leads to the birth of an altogether new sense of self. This is the birth of the self *as presence*.

7 PREPARING FOR FORMAL MEDITATION

The process of cultivating presence that we have considered so far can be approached as a complete meditative path in its own right. Indeed, you could spend your whole life practising and still find deeper levels to it. This is because the liberating state of presence that it leads to knows of no limits or bounds.

The cultivation of presence also represents a good foundation for all other techniques of meditation. Indeed, when these are studied, it will often be found that they offer no more than a deepening of the experience of presence, through opening up new channels of spiritual awareness. In this sense, the mindful state of presence that has so far provided the main focus for this book often lies at the very heart of most meditation systems.

These other techniques of meditation are often conducted formally, requiring one to be seated somewhere that has been specially set aside for their practice. Given that you will intend to learn these, it is therefore wise to first spend some time in preparation for this eventuality.

A SPACE FOR MEDITATION

The first requirement is to select a safe and quiet area where it is possible for you to meditate without undue interruptions or disturbances.

When setting up this area it is important that you do so with the express intention that only the very best of you will ever be brought into it. It is after all, the place in which you will begin to transform yourself through practice of the arts of formal meditation into a more enlightened being. Consequently, it is vital that you establish that space in your mind as being completely clear of all such impediments or obstacles to the achievement of this.

This is perhaps one of the most vital considerations of the meditation process. For it sets up and establishes a sanctuary of safety and protection which the meditation practitioner will always have recourse to. Within the bounds of that sanctuary, the turbulences and problems of one's ordinary life will therefore have no place whatsoever.

As such, it is an eminently safe and peaceful space and in which it will be then possible to meet and make contact with the very best of everything that we are. It also offers us a place to which we can remove ourselves whenever our life seems to get too difficult, complicated or problematic. However, this is not to use it as an act of escapism, but as a willing retreat into a space where our gentle inner life will then have a chance to recover and thrive.

Exactly how this space is set up, and what you put in it, will depend upon a number of factors, the main one being the amount of room within your home that is available to you. If you are fortunate enough to live in a large house, you may be able to set aside an unused room that can then be used specifically for the purposes of meditation. If not, it is just a matter of utilizing whatever is available to you in a thoughtful and inventive way. An area of a living room or bedroom will be adequate, provided it is not being used for storage or direct access to other parts of the dwelling.

If you do have problems finding a suitable space, some practitioners deal with this by using a small rug or mat that has been dedicated to their meditative practice. Wherever they then choose to lay that mat, then becomes their safe meditation space. When not in use such a mat can then be rolled up and kept somewhere clean and dry. It then acquires a certain consecrated feel about it which will aid and assist the meditative mind state.

Whatever space you do decide upon, try to always keep it clean and tidy. This is because the environment in which you meditate will always have a powerful effect upon your mental state. If you are surrounded by dirt, dust and clutter for example, you are likely to have an equally cluttered mental state. For obvious reasons, such states are not generally conducive to meditation.

BEST TIMES FOR MEDITATION

It is also important for you to think about the best times to meditate. Some practitioners like to practise very early in the morning, which has the advantage of setting them up in a good way for the forthcoming day. Others prefer to practice in the evening after work, as a way to switch off and release themselves from the stresses of the day.

Some practitioners like to meditate two or perhaps three times a day, depending upon their circumstances. Here the most natural times to meditate are early in the morning, midday and the evening.

How you fit meditation practice into your daily schedule is largely down to your own preferences, the type of meditation that you might be doing, and the level and depth of your engagement with the practice.

Dedicated practitioners for example, can spend many hours a day meditating, although of course this level of engagement should not be entered into until it begins to arise naturally in you to do so. Indeed, to force yourself to meditate for such a long period of time is liable to cause more harm than good, turning your meditation routine into a counter-productive system of enforced self-regimentation.

It is important to bear in mind that meditation exists in order to serve the natural unfolding of your deeper human potential. This process of unfolding should be as natural and gentle as the slow blooming of a flower. As such, there is no real need for any sense of austerity, rigid disciplines or extreme practices. The arts of meditation should ideally be practiced in a light, relaxed way, and accomplished with a natural grace and serene frame of mind that flexibly allows for your own particular style and preferences.

USE OF AN ALTAR

Some meditation practitioners like to create an altar of sorts within their meditation area, which may be arrayed with a variety of objects that carry a particular religious or spiritual value.

While a Buddhist may place a small sculpture or picture of the Buddha on their altar, a pagan might choose a representation of the Goddess, while a Christian might use a representation of Christ or the Virgin Mary. However, these are not placed on the meditation altar as idols to be worshipped. They are simply in order to create the right psychological links that help to facilitate the frame of mind required for meditation.[14]

In this respect, provided these objects perform this important psychological function, it does not matter what a person puts upon their altar. Stones, crystals, candles, beautiful pictures, incense, flowers, are all examples of useful and suitable objects that might be placed upon a such an altar.

Bear in mind however that too much paraphernalia placed on an altar can begin to weigh down the process of meditation. For this reason it is advisable to keep the number of physical objects involved in the process to a bare minimum. This is because whilst an object, symbol or representation can provide a useful psychological link to a particular idea or feeling, that link in itself may eventually impose an unnecessary limitation upon the whole process.

---

[14] See Sandra Kynes (2007), *Your Altar: Creating a Sacred Space for Prayer and Meditation.*

PREPARING THE ATMOSPHERE

Some practitioners also like to prepare a suitable atmosphere for meditation. This often involves the burning of incense, whether in the form of joss sticks, resin incenses burned on charcoal blocks, bundles of herbs or any other substance that is felt to be suitable for these general purposes.

This not only produces a pleasant fragrance that is conducive to the practice of meditation, but also performs an equally important psychological function, signifying the energetic purification of the space in which the meditation is going to be conducted. This in turn helps to establish a useful psychological barrier to the entry of negative energies and feelings into the meditation process.

The burning of candles is also very popular. Their gently flickering light can induce a relaxed and meditative frame of mind in the practitioner. Additionally, the action of lighting a candle can itself be used as a call to presence. This is accomplished by treating the lighting of the candle as a mindfulness exercise in its own right.

Small bells can also help to create a meditative atmosphere, in particular standing bells with a resonant tone that takes a long time to fade away. Listening carefully to the tone as it slowly diminishes to silence is of course a good reminder to remain present. Small bells can also be used to punctuate the different phases of a long drawn out formal meditation. These also help to impart a dignified sense of ritual to the process.

POSTURES FOR MEDITATION

When planning and preparing a suitable space for meditation, it is important to take into account how you are going to sit comfortably while meditating. Those who are new to meditation, often worry too much about this, believing that the effectiveness of their meditation will all depend upon their ability to adopt the correct meditation posture.

Whether it does or not all depends upon the type and level of meditation that is going to be practiced. In this introduction to meditation, we are approaching meditation as a brilliant tool for training the mind. So far as this process of training is concerned, the most important feature is the capability to sit comfortably in a relaxed posture that will enable one to concentrate and focus upon the activities of one's mind. Because of this, how one actually sits to meditate is largely a matter of personal choice and preference.

Bearing this in mind, you can therefore choose how to sit from a number of well known options that are and can be, equally effective so far as this type of work is concerned.

The most well known position for meditation is probably the lotus pose with one's spine held completely straight. This Yogic posture is so well known that little need be said of it here. If you are able to maintain the lotus position for a significant period of time and still keep your comfort and poise, then this might be a posture which would work best for you. Variations include sitting in a less restrictive half-lotus position or alternatively simply sitting cross-legged.

Another position, one particularly suited to Western meditation practitioners, is the ancient Egyptian position. This involves sitting upright in a chair with the soles of one's feet firmly planted on the ground. The back is held upright, preferably supported by a back rest and the palms of the hands gently rest facing downwards upon one's lap.

Keeping the head upright, one's eyes gaze as if far into the distance, as though focussed on a distant star. This particular meditative posture can often be seen portrayed in Egyptian wall paintings, and the figures depicted in this way are notable for their radiation of a confident sense of dignified presence.

Another well known method is the Burmese position. This is rather like sitting with one's legs crossed, except for the fact that both feet are rested upon the floor. A small cushion or pillow is then used in order to raise the behind slightly. This enables one's knees to rest on the floor, thereby producing a very stable sitting position. The hands are then held together and rested on the lap, the right cradling the left if right handed, or the opposite if left handed.

Another well-known method is to lie on one's back either flat on the floor or on a sofa or bed with one's eyes closed. This is useful for certain types of relaxation or self-healing work, although because we go to sleep in this fashion, it does not often suit the type of meditation where you are required to concentrate for long periods. The risk of this method is of course drifting off to sleep.

For this reason, during those meditations where it is necessary to be able to concentrate and focus one's mind, it is prudent to use one of the seated positions, which allows for relaxation whilst lessening the likelihood of falling asleep. A darkened room can also encourage the onset of sleep, so wherever one chooses to meditate, it is important to ensure that enough light enters the room in order to discourage dozing.

FINDING YOUR OWN WAY

When learning how to meditate, it is important to understand that there is no single definitive way to carry it out. There are many different ways to undertake a formal meditation and, practically speaking, just as many purposes for which formal meditation may be beneficially used.

The proof of this lies in the observation that individuals from every region of the planet and from every age, culture, religion, race and creed have practiced formal meditation. This includes Taoist monks, Tibetan Lamas, practising Buddhists, Sages, Yogis and Rishis of India, the Magi of Persia, Shamans of Siberia, Druids of Britain and Gaul, Sufi Mystics, the Priests of Egypt, Kabbalists of Judaism and Christian monks, all of whom became highly skilled in the arts of meditation.

In many cases, it is possible to even discover and learn about the methods that were used. Having done so, it will quickly become apparent that the word 'meditation' refers to a whole roster of different methods, styles, techniques and approaches to the practice, often aimed towards different purposes and coming from radically divergent perspectives.

The upshot of this is that there is a great deal of flexibility as far as meditation methods are concerned. Therefore unless you are learning classical meditation from an established instructor in the subject, you are basically free to find your own way into it once you have grasped the basics.[15] Understanding this, then frees you from any feelings that meditations should always be performed in this way or that way. Bearing this mind, provided you always adhere to what feels right to you in any particular situation, you will then no doubt progress in a safe, sane and sensible fashion.

---

[15] By classical meditation is meant those meditation systems where everything about the practice is already established and clearly proscribed.

8 BREATH MEDITATION

So far three grades or levels of mindfulness exercises have been considered. These are windows to presence, walking with presence and working with presence. Through the long term practice of these exercises it becomes possible to approach any activity as a direct expression of the stately art of meditation.

Once you have begun to regularly cultivate presence in this fashion, you will then perhaps begin to develop a desire to practice those more formal methods of meditation that are usually conducted whilst seated in a space that has been specially prepared for them. One of the main reasons for this is that formal methods of meditation enable one to enter much more deeply into a fulfilling state of presence.

A good introductory exercise that can fall into both the formal and informal categories of meditation is *breath meditation*. Of all of the most well-known methods for meditating, breath meditation is probably one of the simplest and easiest forms of meditation to undertake.[16] Despite its extreme simplicity, It can also

---

[16] An excellent book on the subject of breath meditation is The Breath (Art of Meditation) by Vessantara (2012).

be one of the most rewarding and fulfilling types of meditation. This is because when we do it correctly, it takes us right to the very heart of presence itself.

Breath meditation entails concentrating and focussing one's mind upon the process of breathing. However, it is important to understand that providing that one is breathing in a natural and relaxed manner, the concern of breath meditation is not with the way that we are breathing. Our breath in this instance, is simply being used as a convenient agency upon which to rest one's mind. As such, the concern is primarily with the mind rather than the action of breathing itself.

A possible disadvantage of breath meditation is that some people experience discomfort and even mild anxiety when they begin to focus their mind upon their breathing process. If you start to experience such feelings yourself whilst practising any of the following breathing exercises, discontinue them until perhaps a later date.

CONCENTRATION AND FOCUS

It has just been pointed out that breath meditation involves both concentration and focus. Before proceeding any further, let us now qualify what is being meant by these terms. For otherwise, the reader may gain the wrong impression when they hear these words being used.

Take for example the word concentration. Ordinarily the word concentration has about it a sense of active effort, a straining of the mind that is often accompanied by a furrowing of the brows. If you try to picture in your mind a person concentrating in this way, you will probably get an image in your mind that suggests this type of mental strain. In meditation however, the word concentration has about it no sense of any strain whatsoever. This is because it refers to a one-pointedness of mind attained when the mind is brought to rest upon a singular point of focus.

Here the word *rest* is the most important qualifier. The mind is effortlessly resting upon a single point. As such, there is no effort involved whatsoever. A slight degree of effort only enters into the process when the mind strays and begins to wander away from the singular point of focus to which it has been consciously directed. Even here however, there is no strain involved, for it is simply a matter of gently and patiently bringing the mind back from its wandering and then resting it back upon the singular point of focus.

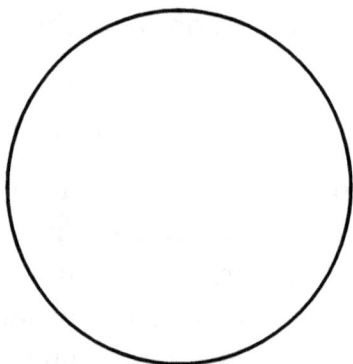

This then brings us to the use of the word focus. Again, the focussing of the mind towards a singular point has about it no sense of effort or strain. As a demonstration of this, rest your gaze for a while upon the circle shown on this page. As you do so, you will find your mind naturally being drawn to the centre point of the circle. This is your mind establishing a natural point of focus upon which it can then rest. Note that this process is essentially effortless.

Now in breath meditation, it is the breath that represents the principal focus for one's mind. Maintaining that focus for any length of time requires concentration. However, in neither of these is any sense of effort or strain implied whatsoever.

HOW TO DO A BREATH MEDITATION

Let us now see how this applies by considering how to do a simple breath meditation. First of all it is necessary to be comfortably seated in your chosen meditation position. Once seated make sure that you are able to sit comfortably in a position that enables you to breathe in a free and relaxed way, without any sense of difficulty or constriction. Towards this end, try to wear some loose clothing that facilitates relaxed breathing.

Once seated comfortably, first spend some time preparing for the meditation by relaxing yourself. One of the most popular methods for doing this is through a simple three-step process of scan, locate and relax. Starting with the feet and slowly working upwards through the ankles, calves, knees, thighs, and so on, mentally scan each part of the body for areas of tension. Wherever you find such tension, consciously relax the affected area for a few moments before resuming your scan. This process is continued until the whole body has been covered and everything feels nice and relaxed.

Once you are relaxed, you can then begin to focus upon your breathing. Try breathing through your nose, with the mouth gently closed, your tongue resting gently on the roof of your mouth. All that is necessary in this case is to breathe deeply and slowly from the abdomen in a steady, slow and relaxed fashion. Here it is important to allow yourself to breathe in a completely natural and relaxed manner. Consequently, there is no sense of any conscious control being exerted over one's breathing.

Having established a nice steady rhythm of deep breathing, then begin to focus your attention upon the gentle rise and fall of your abdomen. If you like, place your hand there for a while so you can feel it moving up and down.

Now when your mind attempts – as it will – to distract your attention with various intrusive thoughts, do not try to resist them or banish them from your mind. Simply observe them in a calm and detached way until such time that they abate and then return your focus to the gentle rising and falling of your abdomen.

When trying this for the first time, you might find it helpful to count your breaths. This enables you to keep a watch on the activities of your mind. Therefore if you then find yourself becoming absorbed in your thoughts, simply observe those thoughts, wait for them to abate and begin the count again.

This count however, is not a necessary condition of the meditation. It is used by beginners in order to make breath meditation a bit easier. Consequently, once you have sufficient experience of breath meditation, the count can then be abandoned, at which point you will then be able to focus exclusively upon your breathing.

Through doing breath meditation, you will find that the activities of your mind then begin to lessen, and in their place a calm and serene state of mind begins to develop. Characterised by a distinct absence of conscious mental activity, this represents a rewarding return to a state of mental stillness and tranquillity.

And it is in this that the principal benefits of breath meditation tend to lie. It is capable of bringing us back into contact with those peaceful inner spaces within us that are usually obscured by the turbulences of our thoughts and feelings.

When you can do breath meditation with a calm and focused mind for five minutes or so, you will have made great progress. Towards this end, try to practice breath meditation for at least five minutes every day, at a time and in a place that is convenient for you.

INFORMAL BREATH MEDITATION

One of the great features of breath meditation is the fact that once learned, it can be flexibly adapted to different situations of a more informal nature. a good example of this is say, standing with your shopping trolley in a long queue at the till of the supermarket. This is a prime example of a situation where one can begin to feel tense and impatient, especially if you are in a hurry and the queue is moving very slowly.

If instead you use the enforced wait as an opportunity to practise your breath meditation, you will find that rather than getting frustrated like the rest of the shoppers waiting in the queue you will become more calm and peaceful. But of course to be able to do this you need to adapt the exercise to the situation in which you find yourself. In this particular case therefore, as you stand there in the queue, rather than allowing yourself to feel impatience or frustration, instead you simply focus your mind upon the rise and fall of your abdomen as you are breathing. Practised regularly over a few months in this way, you may well discover that due to the sheer power of association, a deep sense of peace and serenity will then start to descend upon you whenever you queue for the supermarket tills.

Another good example might be a morning when you oversleep, rush off to work without breakfast and get caught in slow moving traffic on the way. Now ordinarily, your response to this delay would no doubt be one of intense frustration and anxiousness. Whilst the other drivers are getting more anxious and stressed by the minute however, you can use your time productively in order to practise your breath meditation. Consequently, by the time you do arrive at work, despite the you will be feeling peaceful and calm and as a result have a much better day.

BREATH MEDITATION

* *Be seated comfortably.*
* *Relax all of your muscles.*
* *Establish a nice and steady regular rhythm of slow breathing.*
* *Focus one's mind on the gentle rise and fall of the abdomen.*
* *If thoughts intrude gently lead the mind back to the rise and fall of the abdomen.*
* *Practice for about five minutes or so.*
* *Finish.*

9 MORE ADVANCED MEDITATION TECHNIQUES

Breath meditation is a great introduction to formal meditation because it establishes some of the main procedures that will be followed when more advanced techniques of meditation are practiced. The difference is that in the latter case, breath meditation will perhaps be practised only briefly as a good way to get oneself into the right mind state for a more extended formal meditation session.

This therefore brings us on to the consideration of more advanced techniques of formal meditation. In potential this can be something of a minefield simply because there are so many different meditation systems that it is possible to learn. Naturally, in an introductory book to meditation, it would be impossible to consider all of them.

Thankfully most meditation systems tend to make use of but a few simple and very basic techniques that in potential at least, everyone can learn. Moreover, once these are known about, it will then become apparent that they are all based on certain natural abilities of the human mind.

Once the nature of these abilities has been grasped therefore, this then enables you to use them in order to be able to meditate with a strong sense of surety and ease, confident and safe in the certain knowledge of what you are doing and why.

Another great feature about these basic techniques, is that to learn them, does not require rigorous physical discipline, intense mental training or a specialist understanding of features such as the human chakra system.[17] All that they need is some time and practice in order to put them into operation.

They also have the advantage of being very well-known techniques that throughout the history of meditation, have proven themselves to be not only the most effective, but also the safest to practice and the easiest to learn. Inevitably, this is an important consideration bearing in mind the potential risks of adversely affecting one's own mental health through unwise or ill-considered meditation practice.

It is therefore with these basic techniques and the natural abilities upon which they call, that this book will now be concerned.

THE ART OF VISUALIZATION

The first such technique that will be studied is one of the most commonly known about and practiced meditation techniques in the Western repertoire. This is the art of *visualization*. Visualization uses the power of the imagination to conjure up images which are then consciously sustained in the mind for the duration of the meditation.

---

[17] The system of psychic centres rising up the column of the spine and head as originally recognized in Eastern meditation systems.

Generally speaking, visualization may be used for three main purposes. The first is to develop and enhance one's powers of mental focus and concentration. The process of meditation is greatly aided when these powers have been properly developed and unfolded.

The second is to enable the release of the immense powers of one's innate creativity. This hinges upon the vital role of the imagination in the creative process, and the degree to which those powers can be used and harnessed in order to enhance one's own creativity.

The third is to create a highly effective bridge of communication between the conscious and subconscious mind. This in turn gives the meditator direct access to some of the incredible powers of the subconscious mind, powers that go far beyond what the conscious mind is capable of.

THE ART OF CONTEMPLATION

The next technique that will be studied is the art of *contemplation*. Through learning this art, you will have the opportunity to address and explore what are arguably some of the greatest mysteries of our existence. For this very reason, the art of contemplation especially tends to attract those who have a certain interest and curiosity that goes beyond the mundane needs of our everyday lives.

In order to practice contemplation however, it is not necessary to subscribe to any particular belief or religious doctrine. This is because the art of contemplation recognizes that ultimately, each individual is the master of their own particular destiny, which means to say that they are entirely responsible for the contents of their own mind, thinking, feelings and beliefs. Towards this end contemplation provides an excellent and invaluable tool for personal exploration and investigation that will reveal to the meditator an abundance of inspiring knowledge and insights about themselves and the world in which we live.

The art of contemplation also takes a sympathetic stance towards those unfortunate and distressing states of human suffering caused by our feelings of alienation and separation from the natural world, the planet and the cosmos of which we all are a part. It does this through acknowledging the fundamental unity of existence, thereby casting up those feelings of separation as being based on no more than an erroneous summing up of the evidence presented to one's own mind and senses.

As such, those feelings can eventually be overcome and replaced by the peace and serenity of the knowing that we ourselves are all an intrinsic part of that incredible unity, the tangible evidence for which is the universe itself.[18]

At a practical level, the art of contemplation involves focussing one's mind upon a particular object of contemplation, whether this is a flower, a drawn or painted symbol or a particular image. This contemplative object will not only provide an aid to mental concentration, but it will also open up the mind to the receipt of knowledge and insights that will arrive at a purely intuitive level.

---

[18] The word universe literally means *one song*.

The value of this can be understood when we consider the fact that, at an ordinary level, knowledge tends to be obtained either empirically, through use of the senses, or intellectually through application of processes of reason and discursive logic. Although both of these are invaluable sources of human knowledge, they do have certain limitations. Indeed, it is well recognized that most great discoveries tend to arrive by way of those intuitive leaps of the mind that somehow transcend the limitations of both perceptual and intellectual knowledge.

Contemplation trains the mind of the meditator in order to be able to receive these intuitive flashes and insights and then be able to render them into readily intelligible terms. As such, it represents a powerful tool for learning at more advanced levels than are currently recognized.

THE ART OF DWELLING

The third technique that will be studied is *dwelling*. This represents a step up from contemplation for the simple reason that, unlike contemplation that requires the use of a particular object of contemplation, the art of dwelling makes use of an internalized subject. This can be anything that takes the interest of the meditator, such as particular thought, idea, feeling or quality.

Dwelling teaches you how to precisely home your mind in to the territory of that subject, and through doing this, to then be able to receive and assimilate its very essence. In this respect, dwelling is a form of insight meditation.

This works because the subject of the dwelling acts as a filter which blocks out everything that is not relevant to the subject of the dwelling. This means that if the subject of the dwelling is say, *compassion*, you will then begin to receive valuable insights about that particular quality and how to encourage and bring it into yourself. The subject of the dwelling in this case, then becomes a direct agency for personal and self-transformation.

THE ART OF MEDITATION

The final technique that will be considered is *meditation*. Although commonly used as a blanket term for all of the techniques discussed so far, the word meditation also has a much more specific meaning, referring to a well-known technique for self-contemplation.

Enabling a return of the mind to an illuminating state of pure awareness, this experience can be not only healing for the mind, but it can also precipitate that experience towards which meditation practice ultimately leads, which is enlightenment.

A summary of these techniques is given over page.

In summary:

Technique	Media	Purpose
Visualization	*Images*	*Concentration, creativity, communication.*
Contemplation	*Object*	*Stilling the mind, reconnection with nature, intuitive knowledge.*
Dwelling	*Subject*	*Insight, self-transformation*
Meditation	*Awareness*	*Healing, repair, illumination.*

10
VISUALIZATION

The art of visualization involves conjuring up an image or images in one's mind which are then consciously sustained for the duration of the meditation session. The reason for doing this depends upon whether the images being visualized are envisaged as being agents or agencies. As agents, these images can be used to help develop one's own powers of mental focus and concentration. As agencies, they can greatly aid in the process of self-transformation and change.

Here it is important to bear in mind that the art of visualization represents a particular use of the powers of one's imagination. Now it is very probable that if you have not practised visualization before, those powers have not received the proper attention that they deserve. Because of this, it is possible that they have not only atrophied, but have now become tremendously difficult to harness, control and direct. This in turn severely limits what you might be capable of accomplishing, particularly in terms of your possible use of the technique of visualization for more creative purposes. For this reason, it is useful first of all to gain some practice consciously sustaining visual images in your mind.

Although picturing an image continuously in this way is a very simple task, some people may initially struggle with it because their visual imagination is under-developed. They may be people who operate more comfortably with feelings and sensations rather than mental images.

For such people, learning the art of visualization may be more difficult, but with persistence, the ability will always develop. The secret here is to use one's natural propensities in order to assist the visualization, such as making use of feeling and sensing as a major element in the visualisations.

Even for those with a strongly developed visual imagination, the exercise of continuously maintaining an image in the mind's eye can present significant difficulties. This is because our ability to concentrate and focus upon one particular idea or image has been severely weakened and debilitated: through unremitting exposure to external stimuli, from television, flashing billboards, computer games and commercial music ceaselessly blaring in the background. Being constantly bombarded by external sources of both visual and audio stimuli in this way, our minds tend to get lazy and over-reliant upon the presence of these stimuli.

Yet no matter how difficult it might seem to be, this is a very worthwhile area of work, because rather than allowing the tremendous powers of your mind to be dissipated on pointless and fruitless activities it will train you instead to concentrate and focus your mental energies, much as an athlete trains their body to perform in the way that they want it to.

As a sideline to this, it is interesting that modern methods of athletic training harness the powers of visualization to aid and assist the physical performance. This is done by visualizing the entire race beforehand, the athlete clearly picturing themselves crossing the finishing line first. Athletic performances have found to be significantly improved using this type of mental training.[19]

VISUALIZATION LEVEL ONE

A typical introductory exercise for visualization is now given.

First you need to be comfortably seated and spend some time relaxing your muscles, followed by a period of slow and regular breathing from the abdomen.

When ready, close your eyes and in the area between and just above your eyes picture say, a blue triangle. It does not particularly matter exactly what figure is pictured, provided that a simple two-dimensional figure is used. Consequently, a yellow circle would be just as effective.

Having pictured your image, you then try to focus upon that image to the exclusion of all else. Whenever your mind starts wandering, or other images begin to intrude upon it, you then bring your focus back to the original image.

---

[19] See Kay Porter (2003) *Unleashing the Power of the Mind*.

Having pictured this image in your mind, the aim is to sustain this image in your mind's eye for around three minutes, after which you may then open your eyes and bring the session to a close.

If you have not done this type of exercise before, you will probably find that within a few moments of closing your eyes your mind begins to wander and intrusive thoughts and images will start to occur. This is an entirely normal reaction of the mind when required to concentrate and focus in this way.

Every time this happens, just calmly and gently bring your mind back to the object of visualization.

This exercise is best practiced for a period of a few minutes every single day.

As you continue with this exercise over a period of a few weeks, you will encounter various levels of difficulty as you try to maintain your visualised image. In fact, after a while you will even feel that you are succeeding. Yet careful observation will show that even when you do manage to picture the image clearly, your mind will attempt to modify it, warp it, change it, make it move, alter the colour and so on.

This represents another level of resistance of the mind to your attempts to train, harness and direct its powers. When this happens, bring your mind back to the object of visualization for as many times as is necessary. Eventually, with persistence over many sessions, you will succeed.

SOFTLY, SOFTLY

When training the mind in this way, it is vital to adopt a supremely gentle and soft approach to the task. The human mind is an extremely fragile and delicately balanced mechanism and it must therefore always be treated with great gentleness, care and respect. Indeed, there can be nothing sudden involved in the development of the powers of the mind. In fact, the last thing you would want to do is to set about developing the powers of your mind, but instead damage your mental health.

Athletics training again provides a good parallel here. If an untrained person decided to take up running and attempted to complete a marathon on their first training session they would undoubtedly cause themselves more harm than good.

Similarly when learning to lift weights, one starts off with a weight that is easy to handle and then gradually builds up that weight over a period of time. To attempt to lift a weight that a professional bodybuilder would lift could do irreparable damage to a person's body.

Similarly, in meditation one should always begin with the small.

The importance of this cannot be emphasized too much. Growth and progression in the meditative arts occurs not as a result of the application of great strenuous efforts, but as the aggregate of many small efforts all working towards the same direction. In the end, each such effort will always count, no matter how small or trivial it may seem at the time.

A useful analogy here is the process of growth in nature. This often begins with the world of the small, a simple example of which is the tiny acorn from which a mighty oak grows. If we look at the way in which an oak tree develops, we find that it is slowly built up, cell by cell, until a magnificent oak tree is the result. As such each thrust towards further growth always results from an accumulation of many such 'smalls efforts'.

This also applies to the time used for this exercise. Once you can picture your two dimensional image for a few minutes without interruption, you will have made great progress. The number of sessions that it takes to reach this point is unimportant: what does matter is regular practice.

VISUALIZATION LEVEL TWO

Having gained some success with a very simple image such as a circle, you can then make the exercise more challenging by imagining more complex two-dimensional images. Geometric figures are ideal for this, as are a variety of different symbols, diagrams and mandalas that have been used by meditation practitioners for this very purpose for thousands of years.

Once you can picture more complex geometric figures, you can then progress on to the use of more complex three-dimensional forms, such as the Platonic solids, or the natural forms of flowers, animals, crystals, shells, and so on.

This is more difficult, not just due to the increased complexity of the image, but because three-dimensional forms offer additional challenges. The main challenge is the need to picture the form from different angles in order to build up an accurate image of it.

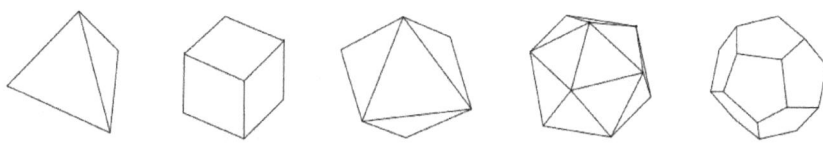

The five Platonic solids are perfect for visualization exercises

In the exercise that follows for example, you are required to picture a single flower in your mind's eye. A useful preparation for this is to obtain a real flower and spend some time studying its particular form, shape, colours and contours so that when visualising this flower, the requisite information needed to build up the image clearly in the mind's eye has already been acquired.

To perform this exercise you first prepare as before. You then close your eyes and in the area between and just above them, try to picture the flower that you have just spent time visually scrutinizing.

As the flower is a rather complex image, you will need to spend some time slowly building up the picture of the flower in your mind so that you can visualize it in vivid detail. Towards this end, try to envision the flower from different angles and viewpoints so that you can see it in your mind's eye as a whole.

When you have managed to sustain the image of the flower in your mind's eye for around three minutes you may open your eyes and spend some time deep breathing for a while before bringing the session to a close.

VISUALIZATION LEVEL THREE

Once the second level of visualization has been mastered, it becomes possible to progress to the third, where the practitioner then learns to build up imaginary scenes in their mind. This is assisted by bringing other senses into the visualization such as touch, feel, smell and sound. In preparation for this, there are several useful exercises that can be practised, such as imagining an orange in front of you on a plate. Imagine the feel of the orange as you pick it up, its weight and the texture of the peel, the smell of it as you hold it to your nostrils. Then picture yourself peeling the orange and eating it, experiencing the odor and sharp, tangy taste as vividly as you can.

Alternatively you could imagine yourself walking along the seashore, feeling the sand beneath your bare feet; the sound of the waves breaking on the shore; the fresh, sea air on your skin and the warm sunshine beaming down.

Or you could imagine yourself sitting beside a chilly mountain stream, feeling the spray of cold droplets on your skin from a nearby waterfall; the gurgling sound of the water as it gushes downstream, the wind gently buffeting you and the smell of moss and wild heather.

Once the point of these exercises is grasped, others can of course be devised in such a way as to maximise the use of all senses in the process of visualisation.

Through persistent practice of exercises like this, you will learn how to place yourself in an imaginary environment that is so vivid that it feels almost real and eventually you will be able to place yourself anywhere that that you choose: on top of a mountain, next to a beautiful stream, in a peaceful forest or an ancient temple.

The places that you can travel to in your mind's eye are limited only by your imagination. Consequently, once you become proficient, you can meditate in those imaginary places, should you so wish. This practice brings with it a twofold benefit: the enhancement and relaxation brought about by the natural beauty of the visualisation, and the benefits of the meditation session itself.

VISUALIZATION

Level 1 Example

* *Be comfortably seated.*
* *Relax your muscles.*
* *Establish a nice slow and regular rhythm of breathing from the abdomen.*
* *Close your eyes and in the area between and just above your eyes picture say, a blue circle.*
* *Allow your mind to rest on that image.*
* *If your mind starts wandering, bring it back to the image. Keep doing this, every time your mind starts to wander.*
* *Try to sustain the image in your mind's eye for three minutes.*
* *When you have finished open your eyes.*
* *Spend some time focusing upon your breathing.*
* *Finish.*

VISUALIZATION

Level 2 Example

In this exercise a single flower will be pictured. A useful preparation for this is to get a real flower and spend some time studying its form, shape, colours, contour, etc. That way, when pictured, all of the information needed to build the picture up clearly has been acquired.

- *Prepare as before*
- *Close your eyes and in the area between and just above your eyes picture a beautiful flower.*
- *Spend some time slowly building up the picture in your mind so that you can visualise it in vivid detail.*
- *Try to envision the flower from different angles and viewpoints so that you can see it in your mind's eye as a whole.*
- *If your mind starts wandering, bring it back to the image. Keep doing this, every time your mind starts to wander*
- *Try to sustain the image for three minutes.*
- *When you have finished open your eyes.*
- *Finish*

VISUALIZATION

Level 3 Examples

* Imagine an orange in front of you on a plate. Imagine the feel of the orange as you pick it up, its fragrance as you hold it to your nose. Imagine yourself peeling the orange and then eating it, experiencing the feel, odour and taste of the orange as vividly as you can.

* Imagine yourself walking along the seashore. Feel the sand beneath your bare feet, hear the sound of the waves breaking, the fresh, sea air on your skin and the warmth of the sunshine beaming down upon you.

* Imagine yourself sitting beside a mountain stream. Feel the spray on your skin from a nearby waterfall, listen to the gurgling of the water, the gentle breeze blowing on your face and the smell of the moss and heather.

11 CREATIVE VISUALIZATION

The visualization exercises given in the last chapter are preparatory exercises that offer useful practice in the direction and control of the otherwise chaotic and wayward workings of the mind. Rather than leaving ourselves at the mercy of the turbulent forces of our own mind, we are now learning how to harness and direct those forces purposefully and productively towards a clear end result.

The value of this can be appreciated by considering the endless succession of disjointed thoughts, random associations and chaotic impulses that run through most people's minds on a moment to moment basis. Imagine that in place of all of this often pointless mental activity there is but one resounding thought that is backed up by a clear image continuously held and sustained in the mind.

The sheer power of that one thought then becomes insurmountable, unstoppable and unassailable.

This is rather like martial arts training. By learning how to concentrate and focus all of one's physical power at the precise point of impact, something as soft as a human hand then becomes capable of smashing through concrete blocks. A trained mind that has acquired this power of singular concentration has a similar capability.

However the essential difference is that in this case the mind is not being trained to function as a weapon, but as a powerful constructive agent that can then be used to aid and assist us in all of our endeavours. Consequently, once this mental power has been developed, it then becomes viable to consider some of its many uses and applications.

This where the art of visualization then becomes even more interesting, because the focus of the practice then shifts away from acquiring the ability to sustain images in the mind and towards exploring the various uses of that ability in order to improve oneself and one's life.

IMAGINATION AND CREATIVITY

One such use, with which this chapter will be concerned, is the art of *creative visualization*. Basically this amounts to the use of the trained imagination for more creative purposes.

The potential for doing this lies in the fact that the human imagination represents the true birthplace of all original ideas, plans, designs, hopes and intentions. In fact it can be safely said that everything that has ever contributed to human civilisation first began it's life as an idea or image in someone's imagination.

This observation in its turn shows that we cannot bring something new into the world, or bring about constructive changes to ourselves, until we have first visualized those changes. Once they have been visualized there is then a much greater chance of those changes being brought about.

Towards understanding how this works, consider that when we dream, we see images which seem to arise spontaneously from the subconscious mind. Although these images may seem to be random and insignificant, they are often imbued with a psychological meaning and significance that is directly relevant to our everyday experiences and struggles. Indeed, sometimes these can be interpreted upon awakening, thereby allowing us a fresh insight into our deepest hopes and fears.

Now clearly this process can go two ways.

Through use of the trained imagination, our desires and wishes can be communicated effectively to the subconscious mind. This is done by clothing those desires and wishes into the form of clear, unambiguous images that the subconscious mind can respond to.[20]

Fortunately, like a faithful servant the subconscious mind will readily respond to those images, and in this way, help us to fulfill our wishes and desires, realize our full human potential and succeed in whatever it is that we choose to do. As such, the subconscious mind is perhaps one of our greatest and most loyal allies.

HOW CREATIVE VISUALIZATION WORKS

The way creative visualization works is easy to see if we look back into our past and see how this might

---

[20] An excellent study of this power is Joseph Murphy's (2007), *The Power of Your Subconscious Mind*.

have worked for us before. Take the example of a person who decides that they need to improve their physical fitness. Having considered various ways in which they might go about this, such as participating in a competitive sport or joining a gym perhaps, they suddenly see themselves in their mind's eye enjoying riding a bike along a leafy country lane.

Feeling really good about this healthy vision of themselves, they decide there and then to go out and purchase a brand new bike. Now, instead of commuting to work on public transport as they had always done previously they then cycle there and back, thereby becoming fitter in the process. They even go on to join a cycling club and during weekends they go out for longer runs and until eventually they find themselves cycling down a lovely country lane, just as they had first imagined.

Note that the crucial phase of this vital change in their life was the point at which they envisioned themselves riding the bike. What followed afterwards therefore, was all motivated and inspired by that initial vision of themselves. Now when this process is analyzed and the various stages that were involved in it are broken down, it will be found to have four respective phases.

First, there is an acknowledgement and statement of the change that is to be made.

Second, there is a clear visualisation of how that change may be brought about

Third, there is a recognition of the suggestions that arise from the subconscious subsequent to the visualization.

Fourth, is the undertaking of those actions that enable one to bring about that change.

Once the way this works has been understood, it is possible to see how and in what manner, that which is visualized can then be brought into actual realization. Through knowledge of this, providing we are ready and prepared to go through all four phases of the realization process, our deepest desires and wishes can then be transformed into realities.

However, it is important to see that this does not work by any kind of magic. It is no more magical than the words and music that stream forth from a radio. Once the forces involved have been clearly understood, all such notions of magic are immediately dispelled. It works because our imagination provides us with an effective language for communication with those deeper subconscious powers within us that are capable of responding to and realizing our intentions.

USING CREATIVE VISUALIZATION

We have already seen that the process of creative visualization has four phases of realization. Let us now break these down further and see how to apply ourselves to them in the process of realizing what we have creatively visualized.

The *first phase* is to deliberate upon the type of changes that you might like to make and why. Once these have been decided upon it is then useful to write them down. However, when doing so, use very clear and explicit language. The reason for this is that any ambiguity in the language used, leaves room for varying outcomes, some of which might not be advantageous. A simple example of this is the man who wished to have more free time so that he could finish writing a play. This wish was then somehow fulfilled when he was framed for a crime and given a prison sentence that provided him with all the free time in the world.

During the *second phase*, which can be accomplished as a seated meditation, sit down and clearly imagine in your mind's eye that the change you want has already materialized. This involves imagining yourself experiencing those feelings and reactions that would arise in you as a result of that wish materializing.

The necessity for doing this is that when we think about something that we need, our strongest emotions almost always centre on the fact that we don't have it. Therefore to meditate upon that need will only reinforce the lack, rather than the presence of what we want.

The *third phase* is to then be alert and receptive to any suggestions and signals that may subsequently arise from your subconscious in response to your visualization. This can happen during any time following the visualization, even on a time scale of weeks or months.

The necessity for this phase can be understood if we consider the absurd example of a man who sits on the sofa all day visualizing himself winning the Olympic 100 meters final. No matter how often or for how long he visualizes this, there is no chance whatsoever of this desire coming to pass until he gets up from the sofa and starts to try to realize his vision. In order to do so, he will of course need to respond to the suggestions that his subconscious might be offering him in response to his visualization, such as joining the local athletics club for example, in order to begin training in earnest.

During this third phase, it is particularly useful to watch out for anything that might involve something new, unusual or out of the ordinary turning up in your life. This might be a phone call from a friend you haven't heard from for several years, a chance meeting with somebody new whilst you are out or a sudden impulse to travel home by a different route. Whatever these occurrences are, try to take up any new opportunities that may present themselves through these channels, because it is often these that will eventually lead to you to the point of being able to realize your original visualization.

This then leads to the *fourth and final stage* of the creative visualization, which is making those physical changes and adjustments that are necessary to realize your original intention. This is the easiest phase, because at this point you will already clearly know what you are doing and why you are doing it.

MORALITIES AND ETHICS

The use of creative visualization inevitably raises certain issues which any meditation practitioner will need to address. One such important issue is morality, which at this stage is bound up with the ethical codes that guide the use of arts such as creative visualization. These arise simply because we have a choice in terms of what we can use creative visualization for. An extreme example of this would be a person who learning about the arts of creative visualization, decides to use those arts in order to try to wreak damage upon a perceived enemy.

Clearly this amounts to a very negative use of creative visualization, one which has powerful moral and ethical repercussions, both for the individual intending to use creative visualization for this purpose and the world at large, which then becomes a darker place to live in as a result of the action of that individual.

Because of the risks of this type of eventuality, meditation practitioners often tend to be guided by a keen sense of morality and ethics. Naturally, these are often clearly proscribed by the particular religion or spiritual path that the meditator might be following.

If not, they can also arise from an enlightenment experience precipitated by the practice of meditation itself. One such common experience, well recognized in meditation circles, is the dawning realization of one's essential unity with the cosmos.[21] From the standpoint of that realization it makes no sense whatsoever to try to inflict damage upon a perceived enemy. This is because to do so would be to create the possibility for the infliction of the very same damage upon themselves or indeed, members of their family, their loved ones or those friends that they hold most dear.

Who in their right minds would seek to do this?

---

[21] The flow of our breath – in and out – is the perfect demonstration of this essential unity. For this reason breath is and can be a direct gateway to enlightenment.

In this way, meditation practitioners often tend to be guided by their own natural sense of morality, not as defined by a particular religion, institution or social grouping, but by the fundamental premises of world unity itself. As such they are moralities that can never really be ambiguous, unclear or prone to human misuse and misinterpretation. This is because they are intrinsic to the very constitution and make-up of the universe itself.

SELF-KNOWLEDGE

Any intended use of creative visualization will also cause you to begin to reflect more deeply upon yourself and how your life is progressing. What do I want? How would I like to change? How can I improve my life? How do I see myself in say, ten years' time?

Note that this represents an important process of turning inwards, a looking within for possible answers to those questions. This is where the meditative journey then really begins to take off, for within it lies a powerful sense that the true answers to the happiness that we seek, do not necessarily lie in sources that are outside of us, but in fact within ourselves: with the way we look at the world, the way we feel about ourselves, the way in which we respond to challenges or with the way in which we think.

A good example of this is that elusive quality of peace of mind that everybody is searching for. Clearly, if we rely on our life circumstances to bring us peace of mind, we will probably never achieve it. This is because the world in which we live is anything but peaceful. Consequently, if we allow ourselves to go the way of the world, we will probably never find that true peace of mind that we seek.

Indeed, peace of mind only really becomes possible when, rather than looking outwards to the world for answers, we instead turn inwards and look to ourselves. After all, any peace of mind that is achieved, is a quality that can only arise from within us. As such nobody but ourselves can offer us true peace of mind. In this sense, by its very nature meditation encourages us to begin to turn inwards and view ourselves as the answer to any problems that we might have. An important part of this process is therefore the acquisition of self-knowledge, because very clearly, without self-knowledge we cannot possibly know what needs to be changed in us in order to improve.

Indeed, without self-knowledge how can we know what we really want? How can we know what needs to be changed? How can we properly engage with our own path of inner development? Without catering for this vital quest for self-knowledge therefore, meditation can never be real, for it will always have to continually skirt the real issues. However whilst invaluable, the acquisition of self-knowledge can also be an unsettling experience. For it is to journey into a overgrown jungle where we do not always know what we are going to find. Because of this, it is always necessary to tread very carefully and with great caution on this particular quest.

CREATIVE VISUALISATION

This particular meditation has four phases:

- *First decide exactly what you want and write it down as clearly, explicitly and unambiguously as possible.*

- *Second, after preparing for one's meditation in the usual fashion, sit down and clearly imagine in your mind's eye that what you want has already materialized. Imagine it as though it had already been fulfilled. Whilst doing this, remember also to allow yourself to feel those feelings that would arise in you had it already come to pass. Once the images have been cast up in this way, spend about five minutes or so clearly visualizing it all in your mind's eye before releasing the visualization into the world with a feeling of complete confidence that it will come about.*

- *Third, watch out for and be receptive to any suggestions and signals that subsequently arise from the subconscious in response to the visualization. This can happen at any time after your visualization, even on a timescale of weeks or months.*

- *Fourth, be prepared to make those physical changes and adjustments that are necessary to realize your original intention.*

12 THE BEAUTIFUL PLACE EXERCISE

When practising creative visualization, you might encounter an interesting and intriguing feature of the subconscious mind; when you imagine yourself sitting next to a beautiful mountain stream, the subconscious will summon the same kind of energies and feelings that would be engendered were you actually sitting next to one.

This response of the subconscious to visual images can be used to distinct advantage, for it enables the thoughtful use of visualization in order to alleviate stress, promote relaxation and create the general sense of well-being that would normally be associated with going on holiday.

THE BEAUTIFUL PLACE EXERCISE

One exercise that represents a direct application of this knowledge is called the beautiful place exercise.

To perform this exercise, first spend some time in relaxation and deep breathing. Then when you are fully relaxed, close your eyes and picture yourself walking down a long, winding path at the end of which you can see a large, locked gate.

When you reach this gate, imagine seeing a key nearby

that you will use to unlock it. Try to imagine the sound of the key turning in the lock and the creak of the gate as it swings open. Then walk through the gateway beyond which lies your beautiful place.

This basically represents the most idyllic place you can possibly imagine. While doing this, try not to let any extraneous thoughts disturb your vision of the beautiful place. Indeed, do all that you can to create a vision of this place that is so vivid that you can see, feel, hear and even smell it.

When you feel that the time is right, think about your gate and return through it, locking it behind you and leaving the key where you found it. A few minutes of deep breathing and continued relaxation whilst you slowly open your eyes will bring your session to a close.

Having done this exercise, consider how you are now feeling. You are probably feeling quite exhilarated having had the pleasure of making a visit to the most beautiful possible place that you are capable of imagining.

Sometimes, whilst listening to music or perhaps just relaxing, images of beautiful places can present themselves to quite naturally, as indeed it is also possible to dream of them. These are absolutely ideal for this type of exercise, for they are imaginative scenarios that have arisen in response to our personal, inner needs at the time. They consequently embody invitations from the subconscious which, when followed up, will bring us great benefits.

Through use of the beautiful place exercise, it is

possible to undertake a journey to any place, either real or imaginary. This especially applies to places that a person might have visited that felt very special to them at the time. Through this exercise, it is then possible to revisit these places in one's imagination time and time again, thereby evoking similar feelings to those felt when this place was first visited. This in turn can help to engender a powerful sense of calm and inner well-being.

Some meditation practitioners even use the beautiful place exercise to create their own working temple. This is slowly and meticulously constructed in the imagination over a period of months or even years. The exact form, appearance, location, dimensions, internal décor and layout of the temple are all matters of personal design. Once built, it can then be entered into at the start of each meditation session. Within that temple, meditation work of many different kinds can be accomplished. The range and type of work is limited only by the practitioner's own imagination. ***THE BEGINNINGS OF SELF-EXPLORATION***

Once you are comfortable with the beautiful place exercise it is then possible to move on to a deeper level of the same exercise in which a gentle process of self-exploration is undertaken. This is possible because our imagination is capable of functioning rather like a reflective pool upon whose surface may be discerned the reflections of every aspect and nuance of ourselves.

As such, through aid of the imagination we can come to know ourselves more deeply, discover what we are prone to, directly meet our inner fears and hopes and much more. In this sense, our imagination can be compared to a theatre, the characters of which are the personifications of the various different parts and levels of ourselves. Through use of the imagination therefore, we can meet these characters should we wish, communicate with them and even bring them into communication with one another.

As an introduction to this art, first decide upon a question, subject or issue that you would like to explore more deeply. Having prepared for your meditation in the usual way - relaxation followed by a period of deep breathing - then close your eyes and imagine yourself walking down your long, winding path towards your locked gate.

Affixed to this gate, picture either a symbol, or image representing the issue that you have chosen to explore. Alternatively you can use a question that you would like to ask, in which case try to imagine that it is written upon the gate and that you are reading it aloud. Then take the key, unlock the gate and walk through it, just as you did in the beautiful place exercise.

The imagined experience directly relevant to your particular question or issue will lie beyond that gate. Therefore when it swings open, walk through it and as soon as you feel ready begin to gently explore the feelings and images that begin to arise in you when on the other side.

When it feels to you that this experience has finished, think about the gate through which you walked and return to it, locking it behind you and then return along the same winding path through which you entered.

Finally, open your eyes and focus upon your breathing for a few minutes before finishing.

At this point you can then reflect upon the experience and examine how it might have been relevant to your question or issue. Then if you like you can write about it in your journal.

VISUALIZATION FOR SELF TRANSFORMATION

Having begun to re-engage with the world of your own imagination in this way, a great deal then becomes possible for you. This is because your imagination will provide for you the very key to the process of your own self-transformation.

We can understand this process more fully, if we think about the way in which we develop our own sense of self-image. All of us have an image of ourselves that has been built up within our mind which is then sustained within our imagination.

The fragility of this constructed self-image becomes painfully obvious when we are confronted by any deeply challenging experience that damages or even totally shatters it, as can happen when we fail miserably to live up to our own high expectations, or place responsibility for our own sense of esteem in the hands of those who do not value it.

The results can be devastating, leading to feelings of being lost, disoriented and confused, at least until we get a chance to rebuild our self-image, preferably upon the foundations of a much more realistic view of ourselves in which our weaknesses and limitations are embraced and accepted together with our strengths and abilities. The important point here is that our self-image has the potential for reconstruction, and undertaken correctly this can allow us to feel much better about ourselves. The tool used to rebuild our self-image is of course the imagination.

Now in most people, this process tends to happen more or less unconsciously; this means that the power of visualization is being used, but without the person's full awareness of what is actually happening in them.

The meditative path however makes us far more conscious of the operation of those powers, meaning that we can become much more proactive in the process of transforming ourselves from our current state into the very picture of everything we would like to become.

This is important because by using your imagination to free yourself from the limitations of time, place and circumstance, you then acquire the opportunity to change your own recurrent history, which in turn opens up completely new possibilities for you.

Having considered the one example of self-image, let us now consider an example of a person who, due to unfortunate experiences in their upbringing over which they had no control, now lacks self-confidence.

Having learnt about the art of visualization, this person then decides to use it in order to instil in themselves more self-confidence. In order to do this, they therefore spend some time each day consciously picturing themselves being supremely confident in a variety of different situations.

Now by doing this on a regular basis, they will then come to perceive that within them there is indeed the possibility for a confident person, one that they can now see clearly in their mind. Moreover, because the subconscious brings to the fore the same feelings that would occur if this was a real experience, this person is now ideally placed to move forward and occupy in real life the changes that they brought about in themselves mentally and emotionally in their mind's eye.

In other words, although they had initially fallen victim to circumstances beyond their means to control, the use of visualization created in them room for the growth of a more confident person. This is the process of self-transformation made real.

One way of doing this, is by adapting the meditation exercise just given. Towards this end, first think of a change that you would like to make in yourself. Having done this, express this change in the form of a clear statement such as for example 'I would like to be a more confident person'. Then prepare for your meditation in the usual fashion.

Having done so, close your eyes and imagine yourself walking down a long winding path. At the end of the path, picture a gate. Unlock that gate and walk through it. Once through, then picture yourself as if the change that you require had already happened.

If you are seeking to be more confident, imagine yourself exactly as you would like to be, absolutely filled with a supreme and unassailable sense of self-confidence. Above all, allow yourself to feel the feelings of a supremely confident person.

When ready, think about the gate through which you walked and return to it. Walk through the gateway, lock it behind you and return along the path through which you entered, this time bringing with you that supreme sense of confidence that you had pictured.

Do some deep breathing before finishing. Perform this meditation every day for at least a week or until you feel that the change has been accomplished.

THE BEAUTIFUL PLACE EXERCISE

- *Be comfortably seated.*
- *Relax your muscles and establish a nice slow and regular rhythm of breathing from the abdomen.*
- *Close your eyes and imagine in your mind a beautiful place that you would like to visit.*
- *Picture yourself walking down a long winding path.*
- *At the end of the path imagine that you are approaching a large gate.*
- *Imagine yourself using a nearby key to unlock this gate.*
- *Open the gate and walk through it.*
- *Once through you will find yourself in your beautiful place.*
- *Spend some time exploring this beautiful place.*
- *When ready, think about the gate through which you walked and return to it.*
- *Walk through the gate, lock it behind you, leaving the key where you found it and return along the path by which you entered.*
- *Open your eyes and focus upon your breathing for a few minutes before finishing.*
- *Reflect upon your experience and write about in your journal.*

SELF DISCOVERY

- *Be comfortably seated.*
- *Relax your muscles.*
- *Establish a nice slow and regular rhythm of breathing from the abdomen.*
- *Think of a question or something that you would like to explore.*
- *Close your eyes and picture yourself walking down a long winding path. At the end of the path imagine a large gate that you are now approaching.*
- *Visualize attached to the gate either a written question that you would like to ask, or a symbol or image that represents something that you would like to explore.*
- *Imagine yourself finding a key nearby and use it to unlock the gate. Open the gate and walk through.*
- *Once through you will experience something directly relevant to your question/issue.*
- *When ready, think about the gate and return to it.*
- *Walk through the gateway, lock it, leave the key where you found it and return along the path by which you entered.*
- *Open your eyes and focus upon your breathing for a while before finishing.*
- *Reflect upon your experience and write about in your journal.*

SELF TRANSFORMATION

* Write down a change that you would like to make in yourself.
* Prepare for your meditation in the usual fashion.
* Close your eyes and imagine walking down a long winding path towards a locked gate.
* Unlock this gate and walk through it.
* Once through, picture yourself as though the change that you require had already happened, experiencing the feelings of achievement which would naturally accompany this change.
* When ready, think about the gate through which you walked and return to it.
* Walk through the gateway locking it behind you and return along the path by which you entered, this time bringing with you the feelings that accompany the change you had imagined.
* Do some deep breathing before finishing.
* Perform this meditation every day for at least a week or until you feel that the change has been accomplished.

13 THE ART OF MIMESIS

One of the great strengths of meditation is that it represents a powerful catalyst for personal growth and self-transformation. This is because it encourages us to look inwards and by doing so, to then discover those deeper parts of ourselves the recognition of which does and can bring out the very best of our human potentiality and possibility.

As we grow in this way however, we will then develop an intense need to access those sources of knowledge, wisdom and guidance that are capable of aiding and assisting us on our path of personal growth. At this point we may then begin to avidly read and absorb everything that has ever been written, expressed and recorded about the process of personal growth generally.

However, while doing so, bear in mind that the world of nature already encapsulates all of the knowledge and wisdom that we will ever need. This is because, as a part of nature, our own inner growth always conforms to those growth patterns already established by nature. The problem is, how do we discover and learn this knowledge? How do we assimilate those vital lessons that nature has to offer us?

One way of doing this is through the meditative art of mimesis. This art was developed a long time ago in order to address many curious questions such as:

What would it feel like:

- ❋ to be an ocean wave breaking upon the shore?
- ❋ to be a germinating seed deep down within the darkness of the earth?
- ❋ to be a hawk in flight?
- ❋ if we expanded our form and dimensions to the size of the universe?
- ❋ to be a beam of light travelling from sun to Earth?
- ❋ to be a rose in bloom?

The art of mimesis offers a direct insight into all of these questions through a direct process of *internal mimicry within the theatre of the imagination.*

Let us now consider how this works.

Take for example a meditation practitioner who is sitting by a lake contemplating the beauty of a lotus flower growing thereupon.

As a practitioner of mimesis, they will not simply observe the lotus. They will at the same time try to mimic the lotus within the internal theatre of their own imagination. In other words, in their mind's eye they will imagine themselves *to be* that lotus.

By doing so, they will then obtain a great deal of insightful information. For example, they will realize that, beginning it's life as a seed germinated in the dark warm mud at the bottom of the pond, the lotus grows slowly upwards towards the source of light above the surface of the pond. And when the lotus finally emerges into the light, its resplendent beauty is there for all to see.

Having realized this it will soon become apparent that in analogous terms:

- we ourselves are like that seed
- the dark fertile mud in which that seed germinates is the human experience
- the source of light towards which we may grow is the light of presence
- the blooming flower represents the perfected powers of the human consciousness blooming into their highest form of possible expression.

In this way, through the practice of mimesis, a great deal of useful information may be obtained, information which will often be found to be critical for our own further growth and progression.

In fact, mimesis can be used to provide answers to virtually any developmental question that we care to ask.

For example:

What is the best way to weather the storms of life?

To find an answer to this question, we can use mimesis in order to study how the tree does this.

First, the tree grows roots deep within the earth, which give it that vital anchorage against the stresses of those pressures that it is likely to meet. The roots in our particular case therefore, are the fundamental grounds of our human experience.

Second, as the tree grows upwards, it remains flexible, thereby enabling it to absorb those stresses without being damaged. In our case therefore, this means finding that perfect balance between the firm and the gentle that enables ourselves to respond with such flexibility.

Mimesis in this sense, is a brilliant way for opening up and reading the guide book that all of nature provides us with.

EXERCISES IN MIMESIS

In order to show some of the further practical applications of mimesis, a couple of exercises will now be considered. The first is called *the seed*, the purpose of which is to help you discover your own natural calling.

Having prepared for your meditation in the usual fashion, close your eyes and imagine yourself to be a seed lying deep down within the warmth and darkness of the earth. Then imagine yourself bursting out of the seed to send roots growing down further into the earth and a shoot that slowly pushes its way upwards. Imagine that shoot breaking through the earth into the light, to form a stem that, as it grows produces leaves. Then imagine the production of the bud as it then bursts into bloom as a beautiful flower open and receptive to the warmth and the illuminating light. Finally, imagine yourself as that beautiful flower for as long as feels right.

A second exercise is called *the mountain.*

In this exercise, bring to mind a quality that you would like to develop in yourself i.e. *stability*. Then think of something in nature that represents that quality i.e. *a mountain*. Close your eyes and now imagine that mountain.

Try to feel the mountain's absolute sense of solidity and immobility, the way in which, whatever happens, the mountain always remains, unchanged, unmoved, offering its tremendous strength, solidity and support to whatever comes into contact with it.

Then reflect upon those qualities, as they could be applied to your own life.

Finally visualize yourself putting those qualities into action.

Through the regular practice of mimesis it is possible to learn very much. First and foremost it will bring to the forefront the realization that our relationship with nature goes very much deeper than we think it does. And as many of us now live in cities that tend to isolate us from our natural environment, these are very useful and telling realizations.

Another valuable insight to be gained is that we are not as separate to the world of nature as is often presumed. We are a vital part of nature as indeed nature is a vital part of us. Through mimesis we may therefore discover that at some levels, we are just like the seed that grows deep within the earth, the hawk that hovers in the sky, or indeed the salmon that heroically battles its way up the stream of its birth. This is no doubt because all of these are the direct expressions of that *greater self*[22] whose realization within represents one of the supreme goals of the meditative path.

---

[22] In meditation circles the greater self is sometimes referred to by the words I AM or I AM THAT.

MIMESIS

The Seed

- *Prepare as usual.*
- *Close your eyes and imagine yourself to be a seed lying deep down within the warmth and darkness of the earth.*
- *Imagine yourself bursting out of the seed to send roots growing down further into the earth and a shoot that slowly pushes its way upwards.*
- *Imagine that shoot breaking through the earth into the light, to form a stem that, as it grows produces leaves.*
- *Imagine the production of the bud as it then bursts into bloom as a beautiful flower open and receptive to the warmth and the illuminating light.*
- *Imagine yourself as that beautiful flower for as long as feels right. As you are doing so, take note in your mind of any insights that might occur to you as you are doing this.*
- *Finally, ponder upon those insights and what they might tell you about your own natural calling in life.*
- *Open you eyes and focus upon your breathing for a while before finishing.*
- *Reflect upon your experience and write about in your journal.*

MIMESIS

The Mountain

- ✻ *Prepare as usual.*
- ✻ *Bring to mind a quality that you would like to develop in yourself i.e. the quality of stability.*
- ✻ *Then think of something in nature that symbolizes that quality i.e. a mountain.*
- ✻ *Close your eyes and imagine that mountain. Try to feel within yourself its sense of absolute solidity and immobility. Try to feel its anchorage upon the earth, the way in which, whatever happens over time, the mountain always remains, unchanged, unmoved, offering its incalculable strength, solidity and support to whatever chooses to come into contact with it.*
- ✻ *Reflect upon those qualities as they apply to you and your life. Resolve in your mind to be as strong, stable and steady as that mountain.*
- ✻ *Open you eyes and focus upon your breathing for a while before finishing.*

14 A HIGHER LEVEL OF MINDFULNESS

The regular practice of meditation will inevitably begin to precipitate important changes in you. One of the most marked changes is that you will begin to become far more self-aware. This growth in self-awareness will at first manifest as a greater degree of awareness of what you are actually feeling and thinking from moment to moment.

In essence, this represents a drive towards a higher level of mindfulness than has so far been mentioned. In this chapter, the nature of this higher level will be considered, together with some of the consequences of being mindful at this level.

Towards understanding these, bear in mind that the earlier chapters of this book focused primarily upon the first level of mindfulness which is *mindfulness of the phenomenon arising within the fields of one's awareness.*

However, this is only one of four possible levels of mindfulness, the others of which are:

a) mindfulness of the phenomenon arising within the fields of one's awareness.

b) mindfulness of one's body.

c) mindfulness of one's thoughts.

d) mindfulness of one's feelings.

Observe that while the first level largely represents a call to greater levels of sensory awareness, the other three levels pertain to a subsequent growth of self-awareness upon three interrelated levels: the level of one's body, one's thoughts and one's feelings.

Here it is important to notice there is a reciprocal relationship between the first level and the other three considered collectively as a group. This relationship can be understood and explained in the following way.

The first level serves to reopen our channels of connection to the incredible energy of the present moment. This is undoubtedly the most important level for the simple reason that it is this powerful revitalizing energy of the present moment that then provides the necessary power, impetus and spur for the growth of self-awareness upon the other three levels. As such, it is mostly with the first level that the early drive towards mindfulness is concerned. Now having gained some practice with this first level, and thereby started to connect with the vital energy of the present moment, it is therefore with the other three levels that this chapter will now concern itself.

Although this growth in self-awareness is ultimately a good thing, it will nonetheless bring you into direct contact with everything that had previously operated within you at a mostly unconscious level. This will include for example, the way that you walk, talk, move and do things, those peculiar nervous habits of the body, the various patterns and processes that govern your thinking and the various feelings that rise up in you in response to those thought patterns. It will also include an ever growing awareness of how you are reacting to the various situations in which you find yourself. Implicit to this awareness will also be a growing sense of the fitness or appropriateness of those reactions, as measured and determined by your overall aim and purpose in life.

Becoming more conscious in this way brings with it many benefits, not the least of which is a prime opportunity for personal growth and development. However, one of the prices that are to be paid for it is oft times feeling acutely uncomfortable. This is because it necessitates facing up to everything unfortunate about oneself that one may previously have ignored, suppressed or hidden. And as none of us are perfect, there will always be unfortunate aspects of ourselves that, when we honestly face up to them, make us realize that there is still a great deal of potential for our own further inner growth.

Realizing this can be very uncomfortable at first, particularly to our fragile ego which may feel very threatened by what it sees to be the gradual erosion of its superior position and status within the psyche of the meditator. However, it is vital to go through this uncomfortable process, even if only for the reason that it teaches us not to plant any more seeds for the growth of those unfortunate aspects within ourselves.

And it is of course with this very process that the higher levels of mindfulness tend to be mainly concerned.

Thankfully, it is not necessary to deal with every tiny imperfection in ourselves that may be improved in this way. This is because *the way that we think* often tends to be the most crucial element in the process. And thankfully, it is very easy to change the way that we think. Indeed, once these changes in our thinking patterns have been made, they can have a beneficial knock-on effect upon those other levels that have been mentioned.

TENDING TO THE GARDEN

A brilliant analogy for this process is tending to and cultivating a garden. Under the terms of this analogy, the garden represents the mind, while that which grows within the garden represents your thoughts, feelings and impulses.

Note in this respect, that the first level of mindfulness opens up your mind to the light of presence, your exposure to which will then nourish everything wholesome that grows in your garden. Presence in this sense is rather like the sunlight that is needed for the plants in your garden to grow and flourish.

Taking this analogy further, we can therefore see that the subconscious mind then represents the soil in which those plants may grow. Just like the soil, the subconscious will willingly receive, grow and bring to fruition anything that we choose to plant in our garden.

Having tended this analogy, we can now gauge the difference between a person who is mindful and one who is not mindful. A mindful person is one who is very aware of what they choose to grow and cultivate in their garden. However, in the case of a person who is not mindful, anything may grow therein, even to the point where their garden then begins to be choked by an endless and ever proliferating crop of weeds.

SEED THOUGHTS

The importance of this analogy is that it shows that to think a thought, is at the same time to plant a seed in the mind which, if conditions are right for it, may then go on to sprout, grow, flower and bear fruit. The upshot of this is that what we think about will always have tremendous consequences, some of which are and can be unforeseen.

For example, once planted, that thought may then begin to attract to itself the circumstances that favour its further growth and progression. If a powerfully negative thought, this could include unfortunate happenings and events in one's life which, when we look back upon them, often seem to have been catalyzed and encouraged by that negative thought.

This is why thoughts of hate for example, can be so pernicious. For they can easily take root in the subconscious mind where, left unchecked, they can eventually give rise to an unceasing and ever proliferating harvest that can eventually fill one's mind with the intense energy of malevolent hatred.

Conversely, if we direct our mind towards thoughts of kindness and compassion towards others, they will also eventually grow, flourish and bear fruit, often in the form of kind and compassionate actions towards others.

This knowledge automatically brings with it a profound sense of responsibility, for it invites the application of care, consideration and prudence to our thinking, and emphasizes the importance of being mindful about those processes.

It also shows us that our thinking should ideally be a mindful activity consciously directed toward specific targets and goals. Anything less is merely automatic mental activity that can potentially plant within us the seeds for much that is truly unfortunate.

NEGATIVE THOUGHTS AND FEELINGS

As your awareness grows you will also see that many of our thought patterns are not only unproductive, but that they can also lead to the manufacture of negative feelings. These in their turn, can then further encourage negative thinking, thereby precipitating an ever worsening spiral of decline.

The most insidious of these negative thinking patterns are those that have become established by force of habit. Usually catalyzed by unfortunate experiences that we may have had in the past, through the sheer force of repetition over a long period of time, these negative thought patterns can cast a shadow upon our whole lives.

Having observed these in yourself, you will probably feel that you want to change them, especially if they keep cropping up and producing negative feelings in you. However, as you become more aware of these patterns, do not fall into the trap of judging them or their content, since doing so creates yet another negative thought in response to first, which is clearly counter-productive. Instead, try to stand back and observe the thought in a detached and non-judgmental manner, heartened by the fact that whatever it is, it can be changed.

Towards this end, it is well worth entering into a long period of self-observation in order to track down those habitual negative thought patterns. Carry a notebook around with you if you like, and when you observe what you feel to be a negative thought pattern, make a note of it so that you can go to work on it later.

In essence, this is rather like pulling up a weed from the garden and planting a beautiful flower in its place. Consequently, when such a pattern is exposed, it can then be worked upon and replaced by a thought which is much more positive in its implications.

In meditation circles, these consciously planted seed thoughts are sometimes referred to as affirmations. They are positive statements that carry within them an affirmation of everything positive, good and wholesome that we would like to grow in our garden.

In this way a negative thought such as *nobody likes me* can then be replaced with an affirmation such as *I like me and because of this, so others will come to like me.*

This affirmation can then be applied whenever one has need of it. The most useful time is when one feels the negative thought arising in oneself. When this happens, it can then be replaced with the affirmation which is consciously spoken at an inward level.

In this way, once one's habitual negative thought patterns have been tracked down, they can all be replaced by carefully thought out positive affirmations. Through this process, in time all of the weeds that grow in one's garden can then be replaced with beautiful flowers.

15 A MEDITATION TOOLKIT

As you do become more self-aware, you will soon come across patterns of thought and feelings arising in yourself that you would indeed like to change. Thankfully, the path of meditation caters specifically for this process in the form of a variety of specific exercises each of which has been devised for a particular purpose.

Some of these exercises will be given and discussed in this particular chapter. Once these have been understood and assimilated, other similar exercises may then be discovered through undertaking further research upon the subject.

All of the exercises in this chapter may be practiced either as formal or informal meditation exercises. When practiced as part of a formal meditation, full instructions for each are given at the end of the chapter.

When practised as an informal meditation however, the exercises can be flexibly adapted to the situation in which one finds oneself, i.e. while waiting for an appointment as an example. In these circumstances, rather than undertaking a complete relaxation or slow, abdominal breathing, we may simply sit comfortably and take a few deep breaths before commencing with the exercise.

REPRINTING MEMORY TRACES

One such exercise is called reprinting memory traces. This exercise encourages you to look back to those times and situations in your past when you were not particularly happy. This could perhaps be a time when you experienced loneliness for example, or maybe a period when you felt frustrated by external circumstances.

The feelings caused by these situations can remain with us for a long while and through creating unfortunate thought patterns they can also influence our current outlook and general state of mind to the detriment of our meditations.

Almost everyone has memories of miserable experiences, no matter how stable their upbringing. The purpose of the reprinting memory traces exercise is to use visualisation to superimpose something more positive upon these negative memories. Having performed this exercise a few times, you will usually find that the power of such situations to disturb your mental equilibrium with feelings of apprehension will be considerably lessened and can even disappear altogether.

Please be aware however that the following exercises should never, ever be attempted by anyone who has suffered from any type of severe trauma or abuse, either as a child or as an adult. Serious emotional or psychological issues are beyond the scope of this book to address and should only ever be explored under the full support and guidance of a qualified mental health practitioner.

Provided you are certain that the issues you wish to reprint do not fall into any of the categories named above, you may proceed with the exercise.

To accomplish it you should picture yourself exactly as you were back then, in that unfortunate situation. Try to envisage yourself as a separate figure that you are observing at a distance, as though on a television screen. Whilst you may note that this image of yourself is not happy, stay emotionally separate from it and do not attempt to relive any of your emotions from that time. Now consciously project a feeling of intense love towards that figure. Then imagine yourself as you were back then completely surrounded, protected and cocooned by that loving energy.

Although you cannot actually change the past in this way, this exercise allows you to modify the negative imprints that the past may have left you with, for they have now been permeated by the intense and forgiving love of your own presence. Consequently, they will no longer have such a negative influence over your present thinking.

This exercise can be flexibly adapted to any situation where you wish to clear your psychic space of clutter from the past. As to which experiences you should apply this exercise to, the simple answer is that you will know, because as you become more mindful the most pressing issues that you need to deal with will naturally rise up in you.

This is because you are now beginning to develop the presence of mind needed to be able to deal with them. In this respect, the subconscious seems to have a magical way of knowing when we are ready to do this, often suppressing particular feelings until we finally become ready to deal with them. Therefore although these feelings may seem to be negative, the fact that they are rising up in you is actually a positive sign, for it indicates that your efforts to cultivate presence are bearing fruit.

Of course, sometimes this process might take you by surprise. Assuming that through meditation practice you will feel calmer and more peaceful, you suddenly begin to encounter the complete opposite and instead of tranquillity you find anxious feelings welling up in you.

This is completely normal and indicates that there are indeed, certain issues that you have not yet dealt with properly. As you become more conscious and self-aware, it is inevitable that these issues will begin to rise up and disturb you.

The way in which this happens can also be rather surprising. It can often take the form of thoughts and feelings that suddenly intrude upon your mind without any discernible outward trigger. Therefore for example, you might suddenly find yourself thinking back to how you were bullied at school. The fact that this is happening now is itself a flag. For it is indicating that here is an issue that needs to be dealt with.

Thinking about this issue further, you then might discover that unbeknownst to yourself, you have actually been carrying around a certain degree of residual anger from that time. Of course, to remain a lifelong host for this anger is not at all productive. So in some way you need to be able to let go of it.

The reprinting memory traces exercise is perfect for this. All that you do is to picture the bully as you remember them in your mind, and then consciously forgive them for what they did to you. Imagine yourself telling them that you forgive them if you wish, and at that point, imagine the related negativity that you have carried since that time leaving you for good. As a result of doing this, you will then find that the memory of the school bully no longer troubles you to the extent that it used to.

Bear in mind however, that using compassion, love and forgiveness to heal your negative memories is a slow and often lengthy process, but one well worth undertaking because by going through it, you will eventually begin to achieve that peaceful state of mental and emotional equilibrium that represents one of the long term aims of meditation.

CALM FUTURE

Anxieties about the future are another common source of disturbance to one's inner equilibrium. Such feelings might be connected with an upcoming job interview, a presentation you have agreed to give on a particular topic, or a date that you have arranged.

By and large, the anxiety that is felt when thinking about these scenarios is due almost entirely to our own imaginary fears, rather than the reality of the situation itself. These fears characteristically hijack our imaginative powers to the degree that we are then taunted by images of the worst possible outcome appearing in our minds. The fact that we ourselves are author of these fears however means that they can be effectively dealt with before the event takes place.

The exercise called calm future uses visualization to neutralise such fears and replace them with confidence and surety. It is best to do this exercise whilst standing since this will not only cause you to feel more assertive and in control but you will also be in a better position to perform the movements required.

Standing upright with your arms at your side, clearly picture yourself in the future situation that is troubling you and compose it as a mental image directly in front of you, as though being displayed on an invisible screen. Breathe in deeply, lift up your arms and push a field of positive psychic energy forward into the image whilst breathing out.

As you do so, picture that positive, exhaled energy pervading and permeating yourself in the future situation that you have imagined. Hold this positive image in your mind for around a minute before relaxing. Having done this you will find that when the event in your future actually occurs you will be filled with the positive energy that you had previously projected and all of your fears will have been allayed.

DISCONNECTION FROM ISSUES

All of us struggle at times to switch off from negative thoughts and feelings whether these arise from our own difficulties and problems or those of another person. Occasionally we encounter people in life who exhaust us with a continuous litany of apparently insoluble problems, or who leave us feeling ashamed or at less because of their sniping, critical attitudes. Negative feelings such as these can spill over into our quiet time, depriving us of ease and sometimes even a restful night's sleep.

Fortunately there is a simple meditation exercise that can help us to disconnect from the perceived source of discomfort. It can be performed almost anywhere, without the need for any special preparation.

First you will need to picture the issue or person in your mind's eye and imagine that a ribbon, or tube is connecting you both. If you feel that this ribbon or tube is entering a particular area of your body – your heart perhaps, or maybe your stomach - incorporate this into your mental image as it will make the exercise more personally meaningful.

Once this picture is clear in your mind, imagine a pair of sharp golden scissors in your hand. Mentally lift them and sever that negative connection. As you do so, picture that the tube or ribbon returning back to the source of its arising, rather like a piece of elastic snapping back upon itself.

This powerful imagery informs your subconscious of your desire to disconnect from the perceived source of your discomfort.

If your intention is to prevent any recurrence of that connection, you can then imagine the point where the tube entered you being cauterized and sealed. This tells your subconscious that you have no desire to let that connection be re-established.

The exact images that you use for the purposes of disconnection do not matter over much: the important feature is that the images suggest to the subconscious a process of disconnection and closure upon what was otherwise a troublesome process.

Having done this, you will then find that those troubling psychic links and connections have now successfully been broken.

PROGRAMMING CHANGES

As anyone who has ever made a New Year's resolution knows, changes to ourselves and our habits are very difficult to make and never happen simply because we want them to. Our subconscious has a very clear idea of our habitual behaviours and will often simply override our conscious requests for change. The use of visualisation however can make the task of self-change very much easier, for it allows us to speak directly to the subconscious mind using the language of images.

Kindness, compassion, patience, confidence, assertiveness and more can all be developed using visualisation, but to do so we first have to clearly recall situations in which we found ourselves lacking the very quality we wish to acquire.

At first glance it might seem counter-intuitive to visualise scenarios where what we desire in ourselves is absent, but your subconscious will respond far better to the memory of a real, personal experience with emotional significance than to an abstract idea.

Perhaps you would like to become more assertive, for example. To do this you will need to think back to a variety of situations in which you felt unable to articulate your needs and have them met by those with the power to do so.

Having clearly visualised this situation in your mind's eye, picture yourself acting in the way that you would have liked, respectfully expressing your viewpoint and sticking to your guns until the other people present in your memory respond favourably.

Dwell for a while on the quality of assertiveness that this calls for and try to capture the feeling in yourself of being assertive.

Once you have done this exercise a few times, whenever such a situation arises in the future, you will then find that you are able to respond in a way similar to the way that you had pictured.

As an added touch, some practitioners like to review those changes that they would like to make in themselves before they go to sleep. In this case, they imagine themselves responding in the required way to various situations that may occur during the following day. To have the possibility for being different, to develop the productive capability for self-change, you must be prepared to visualise in your mind's eye how you intend to be and to keep visualizing this until you yourself then become that change.

REPRINTING MEMORY TRACES

* *Sit down and relax your muscles.*
* *Establish a nice slow and regular rhythm of breathing from the abdomen.*
* *Think of a situation or situations from your past that bother or trouble you in some way and mentally project the scene onto a television screen in your imagination.*
* *Picture the person that you were back then in that situation, and project back to them a feeling of intense love. Imagine them surrounded by this protective sphere of love.*
* *Picture all of those who were involved in this unfortunate situation and forgive each of them in turn.*
* *Visualise all of the negative energy and feelings from that past situation leaving you for good.*
* *If necessary, consciously disconnect from all of the unfortunate or troublesome influences that contributed to that situation (See Disconnection from Issues).*
* *Focus upon your breathing for a while before finishing.*

CALM FUTURE

* *Sit down and relax your muscles.*
* *Establish a nice slow and regular rhythm of breathing from the abdomen.*
* *Picture in your mind the upcoming situation that is giving you feelings of anxiety.*
* *Stand up and visualize that situation in front of you as though it is being displayed on an invisible screen in front of you.*
* *Breathe in deeply, lift up your arms and push a field of positive energy forward while breathing out.*
* *Picture that positive energy pervading and permeating that situation that you have imagined.*
* *Picture yourself in that future situation being filled with that positive energy.*
* *Focus upon your breathing for a while before finishing.*

DISCONNECTION FROM ISSUES

* Sit down and relax your muscles.
* Establish a nice slow and regular rhythm of breathing from the abdomen.
* Picture in your mind the influence, person or energy from which you would like to disconnect.
* Imagine your connection with it as a tube or ribbon entering somewhere on your body. Here it might be necessary to scan yourself for a while in order to find out where this tube or tubes enter you.
* Once located, imagine that tube being cut and the cut part retracting back to its source.
* Imagine the point of entry of the tube being cauterized, sealed and healed in order to prevent reconnection.
* Focus upon your breathing for a while before finishing.

PROGRAMMING CHANGES

* *Sit down and relax your muscles.*
* *Establish a nice slow and regular rhythm of breathing from the abdomen.*
* *Think of a key change that you would like to make in yourself such as the desire to be more assertive.*
* *Picture a variety of different situations where you have not felt assertive and imagine yourself responding differently, clearly demonstrating the quality of assertiveness this time around.*
* *Dwell for a while on the qualities of assertiveness and try to capture the feeling in yourself of being an assertive person.*
* *Focus upon your breathing for a while before finishing.*

16
CONTEMPLATION

Through the practice of visualization, you have learned how to direct the powers of your mind singularly towards the accomplishment of a particular task. This is rather like the development of a muscle and once it is working at full you will discover that you have also acquired an enhanced power of concentration and focus.

Any progress made with visualization represents a very great achievement, counting as a significant step along the way to more accomplished feats. Indeed, once some success has been gained with visualization, it then becomes possible to move up a level and start to learn another vitally useful, yet perhaps more difficult technique for meditation. This technique is called *contemplation*.

However, be forewarned that the path of contemplation is not for everybody. This is because it represents a much deeper engagement with the practice of meditation than has so far been discussed. One of the reasons for this is that contemplation addresses not just the sphere of our own personal problems, but more general problems that have besieged human beings for thousands of years.

These include our feelings of separation from the natural world of which we are a part, our inability to grasp the fundamental unity of the cosmos and everything in it and the arising of those unfortunate and fragmented states of mind that are the symptoms of that inability. Because of this, the practice of contemplation only tends to interest those who do have a concern for these fundamental and very telling problems.

Having said this, let us now see how contemplation works.

THE OBJECT OF CONTEMPLATION

In contrast to visualization, which uses an image consciously projected onto the screen of your mind's eye, contemplation brings your mind to rest upon an external object of contemplation. This object can be anything that takes your interest, from something natural like a plant or shell, to a symbol, glyph or mandala that interests you.

Whatever you do choose, the contemplative object will usually embody a particular idea, quality or dynamic that you would like to explore. The reason for this is that the contemplative object will tend to perform a function on two simultaneous levels.

At the first level the contemplative object will function as an agent for the further development of your powers of mental focus and concentration. This practice in itself brings with it many benefits, not the least of which is a peaceful stilling of the mind and mental faculty.

Upon the second level, the object will provide an agency for opening up those deeper channels of intuitive awareness that, due to the turbulences of our own mind and thoughts, we are ordinarily insensible to. This itself also brings with it certain benefits, one of which is a growing awareness of our profound interconnectedness with the natural world of which we are a part.

As a simple example of this, imagine using a rose as a contemplative object.

When considered as agent, the rose will offer a delightful natural form upon which the mind can be brought to rest. Thus resting, the mind of the meditator will then become more peaceful and still.

When considered as agency, a direct channel of connection will then be opened up to everything that the rose represents.

The result will be a rewarding experience of intense natural beauty that the meditator will find to be not only very inspiring and uplifting, but also very instructive.

THE CHALLENGES OF CONTEMPLATION

One of the strengths of contemplation is that it can open up a remarkably rich sphere of personal investigation and discovery that goes far beyond the constraints of received knowledge. This is because it provides you with a powerful tool for intuitive learning that will directly facilitate your own personal engagement with some of life's greatest mysteries.[23]

Just like visualization however, the process of contemplation brings with it its own particular challenges. One of the most powerful of these takes the form of the *chattering mind*, which will constantly try to reassert itself as the primary focus of your attention. Naturally, as this happens it is then necessary to bring your back to focusing exclusively upon the object of contemplation.

Another challenge lies in the translation of the intuitive knowledge received through the particular channel opened up by the object of contemplation. An experienced contemplator will be able to render this knowledge with perfect accuracy. This is because they will have learned through prior experience of contemplation, how to distinguish the clear and lucid content of their own intuitive insights from the otherwise distracting content brought in by the chattering mind.

This particular challenge can only be overcome by many small efforts, aimed towards learning and mastering the art of contemplation. The final aim in this case, is to have a mind that is as serene as a deep, tranquil pool. Once serene in this way, it will then act just like a mirror upon which will be cast a perfect and unbroken reflection of the intuited insight.

However, when contemplating it is important not to be expecting anything by way of these intuitive insights. This is because the sense of expectancy will simply act

---

[23] In meditation circles this process is sometimes referred to as *gnosis*.

as a barrier which will prevent them occurring. The aim is simply to bring the mind to a state of complete rest upon the object of contemplation. Once this has been achieved, the rest will take care of itself.

As a contemplator therefore, aim only for that peaceful state of mental rest upon the object of contemplation.

THE POTTED PLANT MEDITATION

Because of the challenges posed by contemplation, it is best for the newcomer to begin working with a simple and tangible natural object, a very good example of which is say a potted plant.

In order to be able to use the plant as an object for contemplation, place it on a table or the floor a few feet in front of you and prepare for your meditation in the usual manner. When you are ready then begin to focus your attention exclusively upon the potted plant. Being careful not to allow any thoughts to crowd in and spoil the process, try then to sense the plant as a living presence in its own right.

You will soon know if you are doing this correctly, because you will gradually begin to sense the incredible stillness, poise and serenity of the plant, the way in which it perfectly occupies its own space and its soothing qualities of serenity and peace. The plant is after all, a living being in its own right, a beautiful presence in which the very essence of life finds a fitting form of expression.

The longer that you contemplate in this way, the more intense the experience will become. Some practitioners can spend hours contemplating, while others prefer to spend a shorter period of time, say between ten to twenty minutes or so.

However long you choose to contemplate the plant for, when you feel the time is right, begin to wind down and withdraw your attention from the plant, returning your focus to your own breathing and in this way, slowly come out of the meditation.

Now is the time for a process of quiet reflection upon the experience. This will be helped by the use of your journal within which you can recall any interesting flashes of intuitive knowledge received during your contemplation.

These will tend to occur by way of subtle knowings which, as you home in on them, will be found to contain a great deal of fascinating information that the mind can afterwards translate into words and ideas.

CONTEMPLATION OF NATURE

Contemplation can be practised to great benefit outdoors, representing as it does, a wonderful way to deepen one's felt connection with the natural world. This happens because the process of contemplation tends to quieten the chattering mind, which often acts as a self-imposed barrier to our awareness of those channels whereby that deeper connection with nature is established and revealed.

Trees are particularly suitable for this type of exercise and any contemplative connection established with a tree can prove very beneficial. To get the best out of such an exercise, it is important to view the tree as a living presence in its own right. In other words, the tree is approached in a state of presence on behalf of the contemplator and as presence on behalf of that which is contemplated.

As you continue with the practise of contemplation you will then discover that behind all of the separate forms of nature exists a powerful realm of natural presence. Through your developing connection with that realm, you will then begin to receive much by the way of natural intuitive learning. You will consequently find yourself becoming powerfully aware of that natural sense of peace and harmony that radiates from nature, its incredible sense of untouched inner grace and beauty.

Through practice of contemplation, all of this can be accomplished without recourse to the use of psychedelic or psychotropic drugs. This not only makes the experience all the more real, but it also means that any results cannot be taken away when the effects of the drug wear off. This in turn, then promotes the development of both beneficial and long-lasting changes to one's state of consciousness.

However, because of the particular demands of contemplation, should you find yourself going through a particularly stressful period, a time when your mind is crammed with ideas and thoughts, leave contemplation alone and concentrate instead on reducing the stress in your life. This is because contemplation tends to work best when we are already feeling very stable and calm in ourselves.

SYMBOLS AS OBJECTS OF CONTEMPLATION

As you proceed along the contemplative path, you will discover that throughout history, many individuals have successfully undertaken the very same contemplative journey. Thankfully, a record of their journey was often made and recorded in any number of different forms, whether this be through sacred texts and literature, art, music, calligraphy, architecture, symbolism, poetry, philosophy, etc..

Among these records you will also find a plethora of symbols, glyphs, mandalas and diagrams, many of which were specifically devised for the purposes of contemplation. The great thing about these is that they often tend to encapsulate a great deal of valuable knowledge and learning, all of which can be drawn upon by using these as objects of contemplation.

For this to work however, you will need a drawing or picture of the mandala, glyph or symbol, perhaps even glued to a piece of card, which can be placed upright in front of you.

If this kind of work interests you, an ideal symbol for this purpose is the well-known Yin-Yang symbol, a symbolic expression of traditional Chinese Taoist wisdom. This symbol is both easy to acquire and easy to draw or print out for this purpose. To contemplate this symbol, follow the same basic procedure as you did for the potted plant meditation.

Now at first, the symbol will provide a very useful object that can be focused and concentrated upon. However, after a while, there will come a point when the symbol will begin to function very much like a doorway. Once open in this sense, the meditator will then find themselves downloading a great deal of vital information. This will occur by the way of intuitive insights about what the symbol might mean or signify, the information that it was devised to encapsulate, etc..

However, as this exercise can be very path specific, it is not generally suitable for everybody. In fact it tends to be used most by the followers of particular religions and spiritual paths. Naturally, the symbols, glyphs or mandalas used are those particular to the given religion or path.

THE PARK BENCH EXERCISE

Once you have gained some experience contemplating tangible objects such as a potted plant or even a symbol, you can then go on to apply the ability to contemplate in a variety of different situations.

Contemplation works in fundamentally the same way regardless of the situation or subject being contemplated. This means that the process can be applied to any object field that you would like to work with.

A good place to try this for example is a park bench. Because the process of contemplation is very quiet and discreet, it does not matter how many other people are present in the park, because for all extents and purposes you will merely look like someone sitting on a park bench and enjoying the view. In this case the aim of the exercise is to offer practise contemplating a wider and more diffuse object field.

The Sri Yantra illustrated above is a perfect example of an object that has been specifically created for the purposes of contemplation. Offering the basis for a complete path of contemplative meditation in its own right, every single feature and detail of the diagram has a specific meaning within the Shri Vidya school of Hindu Tantra.

The field in this case is the environment in which you find yourself. As doing this can be much more difficult, try contemplating with that same kind of alert attentiveness that you would give say, to a beautiful piece of music being played at a concert.

Sensed and received with a still and serene mind, the experience will be found to be just as rewarding. For it will above all bring into sharp relief the incredible gifts of life, colour, sound, movement and consciousness that we have been endowed.

The awareness of these represents a true lifting of the veil of our familiarity, behind which lies a much deeper and more fulfilling sense of honesty and truthfulness. For it leads us to realize that we are not separate from those incredible gifts of life and consciousness, but are in fact a direct expression of the very same forces.

THE CHATTERING MIND

Contemplation is a natural ability of the human mind and as such, everyone can contemplate once they know what it is and have been shown some simple examples of it. These do and can include being mentally absorbed by the flames dancing on the fire, losing oneself in beautiful music, or watching the sunset. These are all excellent examples of spontaneously occurring natural contemplation.

One of the greatest barriers to contemplation, as anyone who tries it soon discovers, is the chattering mind. The act of contemplation amounts to a process of quiet listening, feeling, receiving and sensing with a serene mind. However, how can a person do this when they are continually preoccupied with the noise of their own chattering mind?

Thought is no more than an internalized vocalization and therefore merely a form of imagined sound. Consequently, when a person's thought is chaotic, fragmented and disjointed, it basically amounts to an intrusive noise that prevents this process of attentive listening.

To learn how to receive and listen in this way however, it is not necessary to empty the mind of all thought as is commonly assumed, nor does one need to consciously and wilfully drive out thoughts from the mind. All that is needed in this case is to rest one's mind upon the contemplative object in an alert, aware and attentive manner.

Any difficulties that are encountered trying to do this are significantly lessened when we realize that this is something that we all know how to do already. A perfect example of this is when we listen enraptured to beautiful music. The trick lies in transferring this particular ability into a different type of situation.

THE SONG OF CREATION

Regular practice of contemplation will begin to reopen those channels of intuitive awareness through which it is possible to reconnect with nature, the planet, and the universe of which we are a part.

Through this subtle process of reconnection, we will gradually become freed of those anxious and tremendously lonely feelings of being isolated and separated from the world of nature that supports and upholds us. No longer feeling separated in this way, we will then begin to sense and feel from within that natural call and guidance that enables our own inner progression to proceed with surety and ease.

VISION AND AUDITION

Practice of visualization leads to the enhanced development of our *inner vision*. The result is a liberation of the mind through those enrichments provided for by our proper use of the imagination. Practice of the arts of contemplation lead to a related ability which is called *audition*. This is an ability to sense, feel and hear within the incredible harmony of the universe of which we are all a part. However, do not take the word audition too literally. Although implying use of the hearing sense, there more to it. This can be understood by contrasting audition and visualization. When using visualization, the main sense used is sight. However, this does not preclude use of those other senses which will be used to enhance the visualization. Therefore when imagining ourselves walking along a beach, we will also imagine the feel of the sand beneath our feet and the cool ocean spray as it reaches the skin. We will also imagine the sound of the ocean waves as they break upon the shore. Similarly, the main sense involved in the process of audition is hearing. However, as the contemplative object radiates signals throughout the entire range of our sensory faculties and beyond, we will also be using other senses in order to more accurately feel, sense and detect what is being radiated by the contemplative object. Audition in this sense, is a process of quiet listening with every single part of us, our mind, body and all of our sensing mechanisms.

The long term practice of contemplation may also lead to a remarkable experience, one that has been described and talked about by meditation practitioners for many thousands of years. This is our direct apprehension of the magnificent *song of creation*. Representing the original source for the idea of the music of the spheres, thousands of words have been written about this song throughout the history of the practice of meditation.[24]

Those who through the practice of contemplation, apprehended this song always come back from the experience with a liberating feeling of illumination and enlightenment. For they then came to realize that rather than being a separate, isolated entity, they are in fact but a single note sounding within the magnificent symphony of all creation. It is therefore at this point that the illusion of ourselves as players of the instrument of the cosmos becomes replaced by a much more honest and realistic appreciation of ourselves as being nothing more than its instruments.

Through the practice of contemplation, there is a chance of apprehending this song for oneself and once experienced in this way, the track of a person's life will then be changed forever. For they will then begin to feel a direct heartfelt connection with the very essence that moves and informs the universe.

In view of this, what else can be done, but to be still, and learn how to truly listen again?

---

[24] The title of the Hindu scriptural epic *The Bhagavad Gita* literally means *the song of creation*.

CONTEMPLATION

* Select a suitable object for contemplation and place it where it can be contemplated in a relaxed manner.
* Sit down and relax your muscles.
* Establish a nice slow, regular rhythm of breathing from the abdomen.
* When you are ready focus your mind upon the contemplative object.
* Allow your mind to rest unmoving upon the object for between say, five to ten minutes.
* As you are doing so, keep your mind open to receiving flashes of intuitive insight which will often arrive in the form of subtle feelings, often accompanied by images.
* When you are ready, withdraw your attention from the contemplative object.
* Spend some time focusing upon your breathing.
* Reflect upon the experience and write down any insights that you might have received in your journal.

17 DWELLING

Another very well known technique for meditation is dwelling. Dwelling is subtly different to contemplation. Whilst contemplation involves the use of an object that is contemplated, dwelling internalizes this process in order to focus the mind upon a particular subject.

This subject might be a certain quality, idea, inspiring phrase, a question, or even a particular elemental quality. In essence, the subject is anything that you would like to home in on and connect more deeply with.

This process of dwelling can then be used either as the subject for a complete meditation in its own right, or as part of a longer process of meditation that might also incorporate the use of other techniques such as visualization or contemplation.

Dwelling is a great technique for receiving insights upon any topic that you care to dwell upon. Its great strengths lie in its singularity, precision and the unerring insistence upon keeping one's mind focused upon the topic until results are obtained.

Dwelling can also be used to great effect as we go about our daily business. This is done by choosing a particular topic and dwelling upon it at each and every opportunity. In this way, a subject can then be explored in really interesting ways.

A good example for such a subject might be colour.

It is evident that within nature, colour is a communicative language in its own right, as can be seen in the resplendent displays of the peacock and birds of paradise or the intricate concerts of colour produced by deep sea squid . We know that stripes of black and yellow - as seen on wasps - signal the presence of danger to predators, but have you ever wondered why?

There is clearly a whole language of colour at work in which different colours may be associated with particular qualities. Obvious examples of this are the warmth and passion of the colour red as contrasted with the more peaceful coolness of the colour blue. The problem is, how can we find out more about these colour qualities?

One approach would be to study various theories on psychological and symbolic significance of colour. Towards this end a vast amount of literature is readily available on the subject.

Another quite different approach is to use one's own faculties through practice of the technique of dwelling. One way of doing this is to devote say, an entire week to dwelling upon the seven colours of the rainbow, assigning one colour to each day beginning with the colour red on Monday.

On Monday therefore, aim to spend the whole day dwelling upon and looking for nothing but the colour red. Of necessity this will entail ignoring all of the other colours and deliberately focussing only upon all of the things that are red. This is done exclusively, almost as though no other colour existed.

Once your mind has been tuned in to the colour of red in this way, you will find that when you go home in the evening, you will then start to have remarkable insights, not only about our use of that colour in the world at large, but also the various qualities that can be associated with it.

This is the perfect time to write about those insights in your journal.

On Tuesday then look out for nothing but the colour orange and again in the evening make a record of your insights. On Wednesday, move on to the colour yellow, and so on, until the end of the week is reached with violet.

Through practising this type of informal dwelling exercise you will not only train your mind to work singularly towards a particular result, but you will also learn very much about the nature of each of the colours too. The result is success all round.

Knowing about this technique gives you the chance to have fun with it, and to use it in order to obtain a deeper understanding, not only of yourself, but also the world, insights which by their very nature, are capable of propelling the mind far beyond the limits of proscribed knowledge.

Dwelling can also be used to enhance one's daily mindfulness practice. This involves holding in your mind a key idea or thought for the day. A common Buddhist practice for example, is to dwell upon the subject of impermanence. By continually dwelling upon this, it then becomes possible to develop in oneself a heightened awareness of the essential impermanence of everything that surrounds us.

DWELLING ON A DESIRABLE QUALITY

One of the most potent uses of dwelling is in order to connect with those essential human qualities that, throughout the entire history of meditation practice, have proved themselves desirable. Loosely referred to as virtues, these qualities are renowned for their capability to bring out the very best of our human possibility. Obvious examples of these are qualities such as compassion, gratitude, loving kindness, patience, charity, peace, wisdom, truth, humility, benevolence, love, understanding, care, hope, etc..

Dwelling on a desirable quality is a great technique for gaining essential insights about it. Therefore when performed as part of a seated meditation, you would then hold that quality in your mind, examining it from different perspectives in an effort to grasp the very essence of that quality.

A good way to do this is as a part of a walking meditation. In this case, the quality is held in your mind continuously after the fashion of a keyword or phrase, which can then be slowly repeated rather like a looped tape.

One of the benefits of doing this is that it will cause you to interpret your experience through the lens of that particular quality. In this sense, that quality will then act as a filter upon your experience.

If for example, your chosen quality is 'loving kindness', the process of dwelling upon it would alert you to any examples of loving kindness being shown to others that you might see, or situations that could probably benefit from the showing of more loving kindness. It will also tend to kick-start an important process of internal enquiry. What is loving kindness? Why is this an important human quality? How much has my life benefitted as a result of loving kindness being shown to me? How can I show loving kindness to others?

Dwelling in this sense, then becomes a powerful catalyst for personal growth.

DWELLING ON A MANTRA

Dwelling on a phrase or set of words, known in the East as a *mantra*, is also a very popular application of the art of dwelling. Generally, mantras may be used in two ways...

One is as an aid to concentration. In this case, the mantra may be continually repeated in a rhythm that is synchronized to one's own breathing. Either spoken aloud or inwardly, an example of a mantra belonging to this category is *so-hum*,[25] the first syllable of which may be intoned upon the in breath, the second on the out breath.

A second and perhaps more important use of mantras is in order to encourage certain qualities into oneself. To use a mantra for this purpose it is first necessary to choose a suitable mantra. The best and most effective

---

[25] The English form of this mantra is I AM THAT, which refers to the *greater-self* mentioned on page 114.

mantras are those that have a particular ring or resonance about them. In this respect what the words are or even where they come from is less important than the fact that – for whatever reason – they inspire and move you in a particular way.

When you come across a mantra that is right for you, it will immediately ring for you. Where it comes from does not matter over much. It could be an inspirational saying or short excerpt from a sacred text or scripture, something uplifting that someone said to you in passing, a line from a poem or song, the name of a particular divinity, a set of words that you just like the sound of, a sequence of vowel sounds, or even something that you have composed yourself.

There are thousands of such possible mantras, originating from every single age and culture, and devised for every single purpose that it is possible to imagine. Further investigation upon the subject will reveal those that will be most suitable for you.

The most useful mantras are those relevant to what you yourself might need at a particular time. For example, if you feel the need for more peace in your life, the simple phrase *be at peace* would be very suitable. In this case, you would then repeat the phrase slowly in your mind in order to encourage peaceful feelings in yourself. Alternatively, you can speak it out loud. Both methods work just as effectively.

As you do so, let the phrase resonate with your feelings. In other words, feel the sense of peace slowly growing in you as you repeat those words.

Dwelling on mantras is very much like tuning up a musical instrument. They are used in order to attune yourself to those qualities that you would like to bring in to your life. These do and can include anything that you might need at a given time, whether this be improved health, wealth, healing, happiness, radiance, harmony, peace, strength, beauty, confidence, etc. All that is necessary in this case is to discover or compose a suitable mantra.

Bear in mind however, that some mantras have about them a resonance that goes far beyond the personal realm. As such, when properly used they are capable of opening up channels of personal connection to a much vaster universal realm – of which the personal realm is but a localized form of expression.

A good example of this is one of the most simple mantras of all which is the syllable *OM*. This is a verbal expression of the *divine sound current*, that universal field of sonic energy which, according to Vedic wisdom, provides the underlying basis for all manifestation. Personified in the form of *Nada Brahma*, apprehension of the sound current leads to immediate spiritual liberation.

DWELLING ON AN ELEMENTAL QUALITY

The archetypal qualities of the four elements have been a favorite topic for dwelling amongst meditation practitioners since time immemorial.[26] However, when studying this subject it is vital to distinguish between the current scientific view of the elements as some

---

[26] See Virginia Ray (2013), *Meditations and the Four Elements: Earth, Water, Fire and Air*

kind of primitive theory of matter, and the original theory of the elements as the various modes of expression of a single primordial power.

In terms of the latter, the elements signify those great universal powers that ancient cultures recognized as being responsible for upholding, maintaining and supporting the cosmos. Sometimes symbolized by four pillars that supported the vault of the celestial roof, it was always clear to our ancestors that none of us could survive for even a single moment without the vital support that these elements provide us with.

Meditating upon the qualities of those elements was not only a means for offering homage to those universal powers, but it was also a good way to connect with their particular qualities. This in turn served to encourage the growth in oneself of those natural strengths and virtues associated with each of the elements.

These include the steadiness, sturdiness and stability of the earth element, the fluidity and depth of the watery element, the lightness and freedom of the airy element and the warmth and power of the fiery element. The ideal in this sense, was the attainment of a perfect balance and harmony of these elemental qualities.

Inevitably, this is a vast subject which may be supplemented by further study on behalf of the meditation practitioner. This does and can include a study of the elements as signifying the various modalities of the human psyche, as well as a keen investigation of the various schemes of elements used and recognized by various cultures of the world. These do and can include the four Classical elements as recognized in ancient Greece, Rome and the Middle ages, the Chinese philosophy of Wu Xing, the Japanese Godai, the Tattvas of Hindu metaphysics or indeed the qualities of the five Dyhana Buddhas as recognized in Vajrayana Buddhism.

To dwell upon the qualities of a particular element, prepare as usual with relaxation and deep breathing. Then when you are ready, bring the chosen element to mind and begin to dwell upon everything connected with it. If you have chosen the element of water for example, you would think about the watery element and how it manifests in nature. This would include its appearance in the forms of streams, rivers, lakes, the oceans, rain, the early morning dew, etc..

Having done this, then turn your focus inward and dwell upon the contributions of that element to your own existence. This would include the fluid content of the body such as your bloodstream and the fluids that you must drink in order to survive. After a few minutes of this, allow your focus to flow outward again, and recognize that without the support of that element you could not even exist. As such, allow yourself to feel a sense of appreciation for the way in which that element upholds and supports your existence. Once you have finished, spend some time in deep breathing before drawing the meditation to a close.

This can be done for individual elements or all of them in any order or combination required.

DWELLING ON A DESIRABLE QUALITY

* Decide upon a quality to dwell upon - for example 'gratitude'.

* Prepare for your meditation as usual.

* Bring the quality to mind and dwell upon it for a while. What is gratitude? What is the importance of gratitude? Why is it so important to show gratitude?

* Dwell upon everything and everybody to which you might owe a debt of gratitude. This will therefore include everything that has ever helped you in your life.

* Picture each of these things in your mind and mentally offer thanks for their positive contribution to the trace of your life so far. Some obvious examples of this are: thank you for the love of my friends and family; thank you for my health and wellbeing; thank you for the food that has nourished my family today; thank you for the beauty of the sunrise this morning and so on.

* Continue doing this until you feel that you have covered everything that you would like to thank.

* Allow yourself to feel appreciation for all of those influences that have been beneficial to you.

* Bring to mind the importance of those beneficial influences to you.

* *Resolve in your mind to be such a beneficial influence for everybody and everything that crosses your path.*

* *Once finished, spend some time deep breathing before drawing the meditation to a close.*

DWELLING ON A PHRASE OR MANTRA

* First choose a suitable phrase or mantra. This can be any set of words that resonate for you and are relevant to your current needs.

* Prepare for the meditation as per usual with relaxation and deep breathing.

* Close your eyes and inwardly speak the mantra in a slow, deliberate cycle. Allow this cycle to synchronize itself with the pattern of your breathing.

* Keep repeating the phrase like this for at least five minutes or so.

* Once finished, spend some time deep breathing before drawing the meditation to a close.

This is also a great exercise to do in daily life. All that you do in this case, is to inwardly speak the mantra as often as you feel the need to. The aim in this case is to maintain a state of gentle dwelling upon the quality implied by the phrase i.e. *beauty shines out from within.*

DWELLING ON AN ELEMENTAL QUALITY

* *Prepare as usual with relaxation and deep breathing.*
* *Bring the chosen element to mind and begin to dwell upon everything connected with it.*
* *Turn your focus inward and dwell upon the influence of that element upon your own existence.*
* *Then let your focus flow outward again, toward the realization that you could not exist without the support of this element.*
* *Radiate towards that element a feeling of gratitude and appreciation for the part that it plays in upholding your life.*
* *Once finished, spend some time deep breathing before drawing the meditation to a close.*

This can be done for any element or combination of elements that one would like to connect with.

18 MEDITATION

The term 'meditation' tends to be used in two different, but related contexts. The first is as a blanket term to refer to all of the techniques covered so far in this book. The second is with particular reference to a given technique that will now be discussed in this particular chapter.

Fundamentally, *meditation* amounts to a form of self-contemplation, a quiet looking inwards towards those deeper parts and levels of ourselves. Because of this, through the practice of meditation you can come to know yourself at much deeper levels than you might previously have thought possible.

Indeed, it can lead to the recognition of your own true or essential nature, beneath all of the trappings of what is often referred to as the *false self* or outward persona, with which many of us tend to identify themselves.

This process of recognition can happen gradually or even quite suddenly. In terms of the latter, there may come a point where you feel as though you are suddenly waking up from a dream. In a way this will be true, because once you have touched upon your essential nature, a feeling for the intrinsic magic and mystery of existence, perhaps lost since childhood, will then begin to return and as you look back upon your life to date you will realize that you have in a sense, been sleeping.

Once awakened in this way, the whole world will seem far more vivid, colourful, beautiful and real to you. This will be a tremendously joyful and inspiring experience, especially as you will then begin to make contact with the previously hidden depths and potentialities of the real self that you may never have been aware of.

Although this process of self-realization is very liberating, there is also a great price to be paid for it. Awakening in this way can also be very painful. This is because it will bring you face to face with everything in and about yourself that you may have been ignoring or suppressing.

This inevitably includes both the good and the bad, the light and the dark. It is because of this that no-one should even try meditation unless they are of a sound state of mind to begin. This is because there is a very real risk of further destabilization of the psyche precipitated by the bringing into consciousness of suppressed contents that are just too strong for the person to handle.

Suffice to say, this is not something that should ever be undertaken lightly – if in doubt, please refer to the warnings given in the section on Reprinting Memory Traces and skip the exercises in this section.

Assuming that you are indeed of a sound state of mind you can proceed with the pursuit of meditation without undue risk. Yet be warned that the process will still cause everything you have ever suppressed to begin to surface into the field of your consciousness.

Although experiencing this can be very difficult and unpleasant, it will nonetheless begin to precipitate a remarkable, although often lengthy period of self-healing. Here it would be a great mistake to think that you yourself are capable of doing this healing; the process can only really take place when you learn how to stand aside and instead, allow yourself to be healed by the conscious light of presence.

This process of healing takes place because once the light of presence begins to shine powerfully in your life, everything within you that is not in alignment with that state of presence will then begin to be expelled, rather like a splinter being pushed out from your skin. Although ultimately this will be very healing, the painful part lies in having to face up to those unfortunate contents of the psyche that are now surfacing into one's consciousness.

This part of the meditative journey is so difficult and painful that some meditation practitioners try to evade it. A common way of doing this is through the trick of the deadened mind, where the practitioner forces a stifling state of silence upon their mind. This in turn creates a mental dam that effectively insulates and protects them from the inconveniences and disturbing truths of self-knowledge.

Having built this dam, they pretend to themselves that the turmoil building up on the other side of it no longer exists. The self-enforced emptiness of their mind in this sense, then offers a convenient refuge for them to hide from it.

Unfortunately, the illusion of enlightenment created by this method is all too easily shattered when the pressure behind the dam wall finally becomes so great that it eventually bursts through. Inevitably, some kind of breakdown may then follow this process.

To become healed and truly whole again, the meditator needs to directly face up to any repressed psychic pain that might rise up in them while meditating. The hope is that through your practise of meditation so far you will have cultivated enough conscious presence to be able to deal with it.

The key in this case is to let this psychic pain well up in you and then shine the light of your own conscious presence upon it. Once you have learned to do this, like water evaporating in the sunshine, you will find that the pain and the hurt start to heal of their own accord. However, this can be a rather long process.

Having said this, let us now consider how to actually meditate.

HOW TO DO MEDITATION

In the process of meditation you learn how to turn your attention inwards upon yourself. In this sense, your own consciousness itself then becomes the object of contemplation. One of the results of this is the emerging awareness of oneself, not as a reflection of any thoughts that might pass through the mind, or the feelings that arise in response to them, but as a manifestation of pure consciousness itself.

Towards an understanding of this process, consider the fact that you only know you are having a thought because the light of your consciousness illuminates that thought in the field of your awareness. Now whilst most people tend to focus upon their thoughts in this way, practitioners of meditation instead focus their attention upon the light of consciousness that illuminates the field of their awareness.

In this way, they then encounter a higher level of themselves: not as the person who identifies with their own sensations, thoughts and feelings, but as the light of pure consciousness itself, a light that is untouchable, incorruptible and beyond all earthly worries and concerns.

One way of doing this – and there are many – is as follows.

Having prepared for your meditation as usual, close your eyes and imagine that the universe has not yet been brought into being, that there is nothing but the vast emptiness and silence of deep space. Picture a radiant golden egg appearing at the heart of that space. This egg contains within it the concentrated essence and potentiality of the entire universe.

Place your awareness within that egg, safely cocooned, a limitless light of pure consciousness, perfect in its essence, requiring nothing and needing nothing. Then imagine that the egg is cracking open and as it does so the light of your pure awareness bursts out into the infinity of space with the syllable I AM.

Now dwell in that state of thoughtless awareness for as long as feels right to you. When the time comes to finish your meditation, focus your attention on your breathing for a while before opening your eyes and bringing the session to a close.

Thousands of words have been written about this blissful state of pure consciousness and there are many such descriptions of it. One such is this short verse from the Ashtavakra Gita, which says everything:

Abide in awareness,
With no illusion of person,
You will be instantly free and at peace.[27]

---

[27] Bart Marshal (2005), *The Ashtavakra Gita*

THOUGHTLESS AWARENESS MEDITATION

* Prepare as usual with relaxation and deep breathing.
* Close your eyes and imagine that the universe has not yet been brought into being, there being nothing but the emptiness and silence of space.
* Picture at the heart of that space a radiant golden egg containing the concentrated essence and potentiality of the entire universe.
* Imagine you are safely cocooned within that egg, a light of pure consciousness, pure awareness that knows no bounds or limitations, perfect in its essence, requiring nothing and needing nothing.
* Imagine the egg cracking open and as it does the light of your consciousness bursts out into the infinity of space...I AM.
* Dwell in that state of thoughtless awareness for as long as feels right to you.
* When you feel the time is right, become aware of your breathing again and spend some time deep breathing before you finish.

19 MEDITATION AS A WAY OF LIFE

In this book we have studied five basic types of meditation: mindfulness, visualisation, contemplation, dwelling and meditation. We began with the study of mindfulness which is probably the best possible foundation for meditation practice.

Through our study of mindfulness we looked at ways of opening up windows to presence in our lives, discussing how everyday activities - such as working or walking - could be turned into effective exercises for the cultivation of presence.

The long term benefits that can be gained through this practice are immense. This is because whenever we remember to be mindful, the illuminating light of presence can then make itself felt in our lives. As presence is always characterized by an incredible sense of stillness and peace, the benefits of this are self-evident, especially for those who live a hectic lifestyle. As such, presence can offer to each and every one of us a fortress and sanctuary of protection from the adverse effects of stress, anxiety, compulsive thinking or any number of other unfortunate states of mind that might otherwise afflict us.

Next we looked at breath meditation, which provided a good introduction to techniques of contemplative meditation. Here it became apparent that even if you learned no other techniques of meditation, breath meditation on its own could take you to the very heart and soul of true presence. And bearing in mind that most meditation sessions tend to begin with a period of breath meditation, it is well worth devoting as much time to this practice as you feel is necessary for you to get the best out of it.

Next we looked at techniques of visualization beginning first with its use as a technique for developing mental focus and concentration. When assessing the value of visualization as used in this context, consider not only the enhanced ability to focus and concentrate the mind that results from this practice, but also the fact that it protects us from those fragmented, and often incendiary mind states that now afflict many of us living in the modern world. Amounting to a pernicious form of mental debility, for the sake of our own mental health and general wellbeing, such states of mind should always be fought against tooth and nail.

Next we examined visualization as a tool for the release of one's innate creativity. Visualization is not only a wonderful tool for this purpose, but learning how to use it in this way creates a more level playing field, in that it enables one to make use of valuable techniques for self-realization that others have been using for many years of their lives.

Having harnessed the power of creative visualization, it is then hoped that you will begin creating your own meditation exercises, revolving around the particular needs that you might have at any given time. In this respect, be encouraged by the fact that there is no real end or limit to what can be successfully accomplished using creative visualization by an experienced and dedicated practitioner.

We then went on to consider the potential uses of visualization as a tool for self-exploration. At this level the imagination is conceived as a reflective pool or mirror capable of reflecting the precise landscape of your inner self back to you at any given time.

This type of work is very beneficial, if only for the reason that it will re-engage you with the vast, infinite and unlimited world of your own imagination. Our imagination after all, is a vital dimension of the healthy human psyche that if neglected and ignored, can make our own lives seem very dour and dull indeed.

Indeed, our lives acquire a much greater depth of meaning and significance when we learn how to bring the colourful world of the imagination to bear upon the conditions of our ordinary life. For our experience then starts to become infused by the powerful and often inspirational contents of the mind that may be released when we give full expression to our own imaginative powers.

From there we went on to consider the neglected art of mimesis. Representing a process of internal mimicry within the theatre of the imagination, through the practice of mimesis we saw that it was possible to learn many lessons from the world of nature, the knowledge of which can aid and assist us in our drive towards further self-growth. Indeed, through the practice of the art of mimesis we can gain an essential insight into what might be termed the *not-self view*, that is to say a more objective view of the world that takes into account different standpoints to our own.

In this sense mimesis will always present us with two mirrors.

There is the bright mirror through which we may come to know the exhilarating freedom of the hawk in flight or the sensuous beauty of the rose. Then there is the dark mirror through which we come to know of the tremendous sense of suffering that is often experienced by other beings.

Clearly, to grow in a balanced way, both mirrors need to be used, the bright and dark. Through the bright mirror we may learn more about the tremendous miracle of life, evoking the joy and inspiration of all that we are and share in. Through the dark mirror we may learn about the tremendous suffering of others and as a consequence, led to develop a benevolent sense of compassion towards our fellow beings.

From there we then went on to consider a higher level of mindfulness. This is the level at which mindfulness work considerably deepens, and in the process of doing so, propels us towards higher levels of self-awareness. As this does and can lead to the exposure of all that is unfortunate about ourselves, various techniques for dealing with the results of this process were considered. These included the use of affirmations, methods for reprinting memory traces, dealing with anxieties about the future, disconnecting from troublesome issues and developing specific qualities in ourselves.

There then followed a study of the technique of contemplation which required the use of a particular object of contemplation. Observing that this object functions simultaneously on two levels, as agent and agency, we saw that through use of the object as agent, the mind could be brought to a peaceful state of stillness. Once still in this way, the function of the object as agency then takes over, in which it may function as a channel for the receipt of intuitive learning. Basically, this amounts to a process of emptying the cup of the mind in order that it may then become full again. The illumination thereby lies in the refilling of that cup in the form of tremendous insights and intuitive knowings. The aim of contemplation in this sense, is to lead the meditator to the realization of their essential unity with all things.

We then examined the technique of dwelling through which it was possible to home in very closely upon particular aspects, qualities and features of the dimension of presence. In this sense, we saw that dwelling offers a tool for personal learning and discovery that can reveal new insights to you all of the days of your life.

We also saw that dwelling is key to personal transformation. This is because by continually dwelling upon a particular quality, that quality then becomes a direct agent for our own personal transformation. This is because by continually dwelling in this way we eventually start to become the living embodiment of those qualities being dwelled upon.

Finally we looked at meditation. This represents the very heart and core of the subject, where instead of focusing one's mind upon what can be known, the meditator instead focuses their mind upon the principle by which things may be known. This principle is the illuminating light of consciousness.

Curiously there is little more to be said about this particular technique. This is because the regular practice of meditation can lead to levels and orders of experience which go so far beyond the realms of the ordinary, that they then become incommunicable in words. This perhaps is its own reward, for it is to discover within the existence of inner spaces of such tremendous peace, bliss, beauty and stillness that the disturbing turbulences of the chattering mind are then left far behind. And in their place is felt the liberating sense of that *greater self* where knower and the known converge as one.

Having learned about and tried any or all of these five simple meditation techniques, it is then hoped that you will continue with your practice of meditation. However, as this book represents only an introduction to a what is undoubtedly a vast subject, there are levels and depths to the study and practice of meditation that go very much further than the indications provided for in this book.

A good example of this is the art of presence working or what is commonly referred to as *energy work*. This represents a level of meditation that has not been addressed in this book. One of the main reasons for this is that the practice of energy working carries with it very grave dangers which can only really be properly overcome through the guidance of a qualified teacher and mentor who has already mastered the advanced techniques of energy working.

Without such a guide the meditator may do themselves irreparable damage, the costs of which can be very great indeed. To discover more about this simply Google *the dangers of meditation* and then read everything that you can find. This should hopefully be enough to persuade you to find a proper teacher should you wish to pursue energy work.

In the meantime however, as a means for training the mind, the arts of meditation have no equal. They teach us how to open our mind to the incredible power of the present moment, how to cultivate our powers of mental focus and concentration, how to life a life that is free of negative thoughts and feelings and become the answer to many of our own problems.

The arts of meditation teach us how to think in positive and productive ways, how to learn in new ways from the world of nature, how to enjoy the benefits of our own intuitive insights and knowings and how to develop in ourselves those irredeemable human qualities that from the very beginning have inspired and motivated every positive development of human civilization.

They also teach us how to know ourselves at much deeper levels, how to find within an incredible sense of peace and serenity and to recognize that ultimately, we are and always were, at one with the essential unity of all things.

BIBLIOGRAPHY

Abdu'l-Baha, *Address by Abdu'l-Baha at the Friends Meeting House*, St Martin's Lane, London, W.C., Sunday, Jan. 12th, 1913. Bahai Reference Library, reference.bahai.org/en/t/ab/PT/pt-55.html

Altobello, R. (2009). *Meditation from Buddhist, Hindu and Taoist Perspectives*. New York. Peter Lang Publishing Inc.

Ashley-Farrand, T. (1999). *Healing Mantras*. New York. Ballantine Books Inc..

Aurobindo, S. (1990). *The Life Divine*. India. The Lotus Press.

Baktiar, L. (1976). *Sufi: Expressions of the Mystic Quest*. London: Thames and Hudson.

Boorstein, S. (1996). *Don't Just Do Something, Sit There: A Mindfulness Retreat with Sylvia Boorstein*. New York. Harper One.

Brown, Kirk Warren; Ryan, Richard M (2004), The Benefits of Being Present: Mindfulness and its Role in Psychological Well-being. *Journal of Psychosomatic Research*. Volume 57, Issue 1, July 2004, Pages 35 – 43.

Brown, Kirk Warren; Ryan, Richard M. The benefits of being present: mindfulness and its role in psychological well-being. *Journal of Personality and Social Psychology*, Vol 84(4), Apr 2003, 822-848.

Chinmoy, S. (2011). *Meditation: Man-Perfection in God-Satisfaction*. Aum Publications.

Chopra, D. (1994). *Journey Into Healing: Awakening the Wisdom Within You.* U.S. Harmony Books.

Chopra, D. (2013), Meditation has Nothing to do with Religion. *HuffingtonPost.* www. huffingtonpost. Com /2013/02/05/meditation-deepak-chopra_n_2600707.html

Dyson, Freeman (1981). *Disturbing the Universe.* New York. Basic Books.

Gawain, S. (2002). *Creative Visualization.* Novato. Nataraj Publishing.

Gelles, D. (2015). *Mindful Work: How Meditation is Changing Businesses from the Inside Out.* London. Profile Books.

Grossman, P.; Niemann, L. Schmidt, S. (2004). Mindfulness-based Stress Reduction and Health Benefits: a Meta Analysis. *Journal of Personality and Social Psychology*, Vol 84 (4), April 2003, 822-848.

Hine, J. (2014). *Tai Chi and Mindfulness.* Taichi-europe.com

Hofmann, S.G.. Sawyer, A.T., Witt, A.A., & Oh, D. (2010). The effect of mindfulness-based therapy on anxiety and depression: A meta-analytic review. *Journal of Consulting & Clinical Psychology*, 78(2), 169-183.

Khan, H. I. *Mental Purification and Healing, Part III: Mental Purification,* Chapter XV, THE SECRET OF BREATH. http://wahiduddin.net/mv2/IV/IV_32.htm.

Kynes. S (2007). *Your Altar: Creating a Sacred Space for Prayer and Meditation.* U.S. Llewellyn Publications.

Mascaro, J. (1982). *The Bhagavad Gita.* London. Penguin Classics.

Marshal, B. (2005). *Ashtavakra Gita.* Online Ed.

Moore, Thomas. (1993). *Care of the Soul.* New York. HarperCollins.

Murphy, J. (2007). *The Power of Your Subconscious Mind.* New York. Dover Publications Inc..

Porter, K. (2003). *The Mental Athlete: Inner Training for Peak Performance in All Sports.* Champaign, Human Kinetics.

Rama, Swami (2009). *Science of Breath: A Practical Guide.* Himalayan Institute Press.

Ravindra, Ravi (2012). *The Wisdom of Patanjali's Yoga Sutra: A New Translation and Guide by Ravi Ravindra.* India. The Theosophical Publishing House.

Ray, Amit (2010), *Om Chanting and Meditation.* Rishikesh. Inner Light Publishers.

Ray, Amit (2012). *Yoga and Vipassana: An Integrated Lifestyle.* Rishikesh. Inner Light Publishers.

Ray, Virginia. (2013). *Meditations and the Four Elements: Earth, Water, Fire and Air.* Createspace Independent Publishing Platform.

Rinpoche, S. (2008). *The Tibetan Book Of Living And Dying: A Spiritual Classic from One of the Foremost Interpreters of Tibetan Buddhism to the West* (Rider 100). London. Ryder Classics

Slingerland, E. (2006). *Effortless Action: Wu-wei As Conceptual Metaphor and Spiritual Ideal in Early China*. London. Oxford University Press.

Stapely, L. (2015). *The Power of Affirmations*. Createspace Independent Publishing Platform.

The Gaian Dragon http://www.jamesclairlewis.com/

Thich Nhat Hanh & Anh-Huong Nguyen, (2006). *Walking Meditation*. Sounds True Inc.

Tolle, E. (2001). *The Power of Now*. London. Hodder and Stoughton.

Vessantara, (2012). *The Breath - Art of Meditation*. London. Windhorse Publications Ltd.

Watts, Alan (1989). *The Book: On the Taboo against Knowing Who You Really Are*. NewYork. Vintage Books.

Williams, M. (2011). *Mindfulness: A Practical Guide to Finding Peace in a Frantic World*. London. Piatkus Publishers.

INDEX

affirmations, 123, 176
altar, 53, 54
ancient cultures, 160
ancient Egyptian position, 57
ancient temple, 83
anticipation., 25, 26
anxiety, 7, 47, 61, 129, 135, 173, 181
anxious feelings, 128, 150
art of visualization, 75, 104
Ashtavakra Gita, 171, 182
assertiveness, 130, 132, 133, 137
atheist, 24
athletic training, 77
audition, 12
automatic mental activity, 122
beautiful music, 148, 150
beautiful stream, 83
beauty, 20, 21, 37, 44, 83, 140, 144, 162, 176
bells, 55
benevolence, 156
breath meditation, 60-7, 174
breathing, 14, 36, 61, 63, 64, 65, 67, 77, 84, 102, 106, 107, 114, 115, 116, 125, 130, 134, 135, 136, 137, 143, 152, 164, 171, 172
Buddhism, 6, 7, 54. 57. 155, 180, 182
Burmese position, 57

calling, 24, 112, 114
candles, 54, 55
care, 45, 79, 122, 153, 156
communication, 70, 74, 91
celestial roof, 160
chakra system, 69
charity, 156
Christ, 54
Christian monks, 58
classical meditation, 59
colour, 78, 147, 154, 155
compassion, 122, 129, 132, 156, 176
compassionate actions, 122
concentration, 74
confidence, 97, 105, 130, 132
conscious mental activity, 65
consciousness, 147, 167, 169, 170, 172, 176, 178
contemplation, 3, 70, 71, 72, 138, 139, 140, 141, 142, 143, 144, 146, 147, 148, 150, 151, 152, 153, 166, 169, 173, 177
contemplative meditation, 2, 34, 146, 173
contemplative path, 144
conversation, 27, 28, 33
creative process, 70, 75
creative visualization, 91, 93, 94, 175

creativity, 70, 74, 174
cultivate presence, 128
current outlook, 126
daydreams, 26, 32, 36
deep breathing, 64, 81, 98, 99, 101, 105, 108, 161, 163, 164, 165, 172
disconnection, 131
dreaming, 89
Druids of Britain and Gaul, 58
dwelling, 3, 52, 72, 73, 153, 154, 155, 156, 157, 159, 173, 177
ego, 119
Egyptian wall paintings, 57
elemental qualities, 159
enlightenment, 73, 94, 151, 169
essential nature, 166
ethical codes, 93
falling asleep, 58
familiarity, 47, 147
feelings of separation, 71
focused mind, 65
forest, 83
formal meditation, 55, 58, 125
geometric figures, 80
Goddess, 54
gratitude, 156, 162, 165
habitual behaviours, 132
half-lotus position, 56
happiness, 95
harmony, 144
hate, 121
healing, 11, 57, 71, 73, 168
heightened awareness, 156
hope, 21, 47, 156, 169
human potential, 53, 89
humility, 156
idyllic situation, 99
illumination, 74, 151, 177
imaginary environment, 82
imaginary fears, 129
imaginary places, 83
imagination, 75, 76, 83, 89, 91, 100, 102, 103, 110, 134
imaginative powers, 129, 175
incense, 54, 55
insight, 74
insights, 38, 73, 114, 152, 153, 155, 156, 177
interconnectedness, 140
intergalactic space, 29
intuition, 71, 72, 74, 132, 139, 140, 141, 143, 144, 150, 152, 177
intuitive insights, 141
Kabbalists, 58
knowledge, 71, 72, 74, 96, 122, 140, 141, 143, 155, 168
loose clothing, 63
lotus pose, 56
love, 127, 129, 134, 156, 162
loving kindness, 157
Magi of Persia, 58
mandalas, 80, 145
mantra, 157, 158, 164
martial arts, 87
meditation area, 53
meditation posture, 56
meditation practice, 69, 173

meditative path, 50, 103
mental concentration, 71
mental cultivation, 23, 24
mental equilibrium, 126
mental faculty, 139
mental focus, 70, 75, 139, 174
mental image, 130, 131
mimesis, 110, 111, 175, 176
mind's eye, 76, 77, 81, 83, 84, 85, 90, 92, 97, 104, 131, 133, 139
mindfulness, 1, 2, 4, 6, 7, 8, 9, 11, 13, 25, 27, 28, 32, 33, 47, 49, 60, 117, 118, 120, 155, 173, 176, 181
mindfulness practice, 2, 4, 6, 25, 28, 155
moralities, 93
mountain,, 83, 116
music of the spheres, 150
mysteries, 70, 140
Nada Brahma, 159
natural call, 150
natural world, 71, 143, 154
negative energies, 55
negative feelings, 42
negative thoughts, 130
negative thought, 121
non-action, 9, 21
object of contemplation, 71, 72, 139, 141, 177
OM, 159
outward persona, 166
patience, 132, 156
peace, 29, 30, 33, 66, 71, 95, 96, 142, 144, 156, 158, 171, 173, 178
peace of mind, 96
peaceful inner spaces, 65
personal growth, 119
personal investigation, 140
physical fitness, 90
Platonic solids, 80, 81
positive psychic energy, 130
practising Buddhists, 58
preparatory exercises, 87
presence, 8, 9, 11, 13, 16, 19, 20, 21, 22, 34, 36, 37, 38, 41, 42, 44, 45, 49, 50, 55, 57, 60, 76, 92, 120, 127, 142, 143, 144, 154, 168, 169, 173, 174, 177, 178
present moment, 7, 8, 9, 11, 20, 21, 22, 36, 37, 47, 48, 118
Priests of Egypt, 58
primordial power, 160
psychic links, 132
psychotropic drugs, 144
pure awareness, 73, 170, 172
purpose in life, 119
quality, 6, 8, 29, 44, 72, 95, 96, 112, 116, 132, 137, 139, 153, 156, 157, 162, 177
reconnection, 74, 136, 150
reconnection with nature, 74
recurrent history, 103
relaxation, 57, 58, 63, 77, 83, 98, 99, 101, 125, 130, 161, 164, 165, 172
religious doctrine, 70

reprinting memory traces, 126, 129, 176
Rishis of India, 58
sacred text, 158
Sages, 58
self discovery, 107
self-awareness, 117, 118, 176
self-change, 132, 133
self-confidence, 103, 104, 105
self-exploration, 100, 175
self-image, 102, 103
self-knowledge, 96
self-realization, 167, 174
self-transformation, 73, 75, 102, 104
sensory awareness, 117, 118
Shamans of Siberia, 58
Shri Vidya school, 146
silence, 30, 31, 33, 55, 168, 170, 172
sleep, 57, 58, 131, 133
small efforts, 79, 141
song of creation, 150
sonic energy, 159
sound current, 159
spiritual awareness, 50
spiritual liberation, 159
spiritual pathway, 7
Sri Yantra, 146
standing bells, 55
stardust, 21, 22
state of consciousness, 144
state of mind, 5, 23, 65, 126, 167
state of presence, 8, 22, 41, 49, 50, 60, 143, 168
stilling the mind, 74
stillness, 29, 30, 33, 65, 142, 173, 177, 178
stress, 48, 49, 98, 173
subconscious, 70, 89, 91, 92, 93, 97, 98, 99, 104, 120, 121, 127, 131, 132
subconscious mind, 70, 89, 98, 120, 121, 132
Sufi Mystics, 58
symbol, 30, 54, 71, 101, 107, 139, 145, 146
symbols, 80, 145
Tai Chi, 8, 181
Taoism, 6
Taoist monks, 58
the beautiful place exercise, 98, 99, 100, 101
the chariot, 23, 24
the cosmos, 71, 94, 151, 160
the elements, 159, 160, 161
the false self, 166
the garden, 120
the heron, 11
the imagination, 69, 70, 100, 103, 110, 175
the real self, 167
the universe, 71, 110, 150, 170, 172
the chattering mind, 141, 143, 148, 178
thought patterns, 49, 119, 126
thoughtless awareness, 172
Tibetan Lamas, 58
times to meditate, 52, 53
understanding, 69, 117, 155, 156, 169

unfortunate aspects, 119
unity, 71, 94, 177
unity of existence, 71
universal powers, 160
Vedic lore, 159
Virgin Mary, 54
vision, 92, 99
visualization, 3, 69, 75, 76, 77, 78, 81, 82, 87, 88, 91, 92, 93, 94, 95, 97, 98, 103, 104, 130, 138, 139, 140, 153, 174, 175
vowel sounds, 158

walking with presence, 42, 60
ways of thinking, 120
well-being, 6, 98, 100, 180
Western culture, 6
wisdom, 156
working with presence, 42, 60
world of nature, 140, 175
Wu Wei, 8, 9, 21
Yogis, 58
Zen Buddhism, 6